BURGOYNE'S CAMPAIGN,

KENNIKAT AMERICAN BICENTENNIAL SERIES
Under the General Editorial Supervision of
Dr. Ralph Adams Brown
Professor of History, State University of New York

AN

Original, Compiled and Corrected Account

OF

BURGOYNE'S CAMPAIGN,

AND THE

MEMORABLE BATTLES OF BEMIS'S HEIGHTS,

SEPT. 19, AND OCT. 7, 1777,

FROM THE MOST AUTHENTIC SOURCES OF INFORMATION;

INCLUDING

MANY INTERESTING INCIDENTS

CONNECTED WITH THE SAME:

BY CHARLES NEILSON, ESQ.

Methinks I hear the sound of time long past
Still murmuring o'er me, and whispering in
The following pages—like the lingering voices
Of those who long within their graves have slept.

KENNIKAT PRESS
Port Washington, N. Y./London

BURGOYNE'S CAMPAIGN

First published in 1844, 1926
Reissued in 1970 by Kennikat Press
Library of Congress Catalog Card No: 70-120888
ISBN 0-8046-1281-1

Manufactured by Taylor Publishing Company   Dallas, Texas

KENNIKAT AMERICAN BICENTENNIAL SERIES

RECOMMENDATIONS.

The following Recommendation is from the Rev. Charles O. Kimball, and the Rev. Isaac Wescott.

STILLWATER, MARCH 28, 1844.

CHARLES NEILSON, ESQ:

Dear Sir—We have read with deep interest your work in manuscript entitled "An Original, Compiled and Corrected Account of Burgoyne's Campaign, and the Memorable Battles on Bemis's Heights, on the 19th September, and 7th October, 1777" &c. &c., and are free to say, that we believe it to be a document of great merit, containing a full, clear, and authentic statement of important facts and incidents, of the most thrilling kind, connected with the Revolutionary war.

The book is eminently worthy of publication, and introduction into every family in the country, and of being read by every youth, that the rising generation may enjoy the correct, interesting and profitable view therein presented, of the toils, sufferings, conflicts, and triumphs of our venerable ancestors. The ability, age, and above all, the peculiarly favorable circumstances of the author's birth, education, and parentage, exhibit the most lucid proof of qualification for the work, and sure evidence of truth and fidelity in its execution.

These circumstances should secure a ready and extensive sale.

With sentiments of respect and esteem,
Permit us, sir, to subscribe ourselves,
Your obedient servants,
CHARLES O. KIMBALL.
ISAAC WESCOTT.

ALBANY, May 23, 1844.

CHARLES NEILSON, ESQ.,

Dear Sir—At your request, and that of my esteemed friend,

the Rev. Mr. Kimball of Stillwater, I have perused most of the proof sheets of your "Account of Burgoyne's Campaign and of the Memorable Battles of Bemis's Heights," and I can truly say, that I have derived much pleasure as well as information from their perusal. Without intending to pass upon the comparative accuracy of your account of this portion of our Revolutionary history, and those of your predecessors, or to sit in judgment upon the motives which governed the conduct of some of the principal agents connected with the transactions of this important campaign, I cheerfully accord to you, the credit which I think you richly deserve, of having materially, and in an attractive form, added to our stock of historical information, in reference to a period big with the future destinies and fate of our beloved country.

Very respectfully,
Your obedient servant,
SAMUEL S. RANDALL.

TO A PATRIOTIC PUBLIC.

As the memorable battles on Bemis's Heights have become a subject of increasing interest to the "good people" of these United States; and as no historian, in his own account of the revolutionary war, has yet given a very minute or even *correct* superficial account of the same, it has been suggested by many, who feel a deep interest in the subject, that a more particular history ought to be given to the public, for the benefit of the present, rising, and all future generations; accompanied with a topographical view, or description of the important ground, and its relative situation with respect to the surrounding country; and is the simple reason for even *commencing* the following narrative.

The author, in the absence of some one better qualified for the important duty, though he knows his own efforts will be feeble and inadequate to the task, has thought proper, as far as in him lies, to *try* to give a true and impartial history of all, or at least, the principal facts relative to the several movements of the two armies under generals Gates and Burgoyne, and of the several battles fought between different portions of the same, according to the most authentic information that, he thinks at least, can possibly be obtained at this, so late a day. As the author is not writing to please any particular individual or set of men, or to gratify the peculiar taste of any particular class of readers, he will not, therefore, as far as his own style is used, attempt to dress his subject in lofty and sublime language, or in unintelligible and mysterious phrases, but in the plain and simple every-day language of a humble *farmer,* as he is, and in language, he hopes, that will be understood equally as well by the common school boy, as by the man of science. In giving an account of any important transaction that took place at some remote former period, it is always desirable, and sometimes thought necessary, especially when there has been so many different accounts of the same transaction, as in this case, that the author introduce some facts or circumstances connected with the subject under consideration, that will have a tendency at least, to place the narrative beyond the possibility of doubt.

In respect to the topographical description, the author refers the reader to an examination of the ground thereon described, where he will not only find a great portion of the remains of the old entrenchments and other fortifications, as evidence of its correctness, but will, he thinks, be much gratified with a view from the author's dwelling—of the most beautiful, picturesque, and extensive landscape to be found, perhaps, within the "Empire State."

If taste for grandeur, or the more sublime,
Prompt thee, my friend, these gentle Heights to climb,
Here gaze attentive on the scene around,
But tread, with holy awe, this hallow'd ground!

In order that the reader may the better judge of the authenticity of the author's information on the subject on which he is about to write, he will remark, that in addition to the information repeatedly received from a number of the old revolutionary officers and soldiers, who have ever resided in this vicinity, and who took a part in the battles; he also received it from his much respected father, a man of well known strong and discerning mind, of superior intellect, and the most retentive memory, who lived at the time of those most important events, within the circle of the American camp on Bemis's Heights, and in the very house, now standing, in which the brave Gen. Poor and the heroic Col. Morgan quartered; and who was a volunteer under Gen. Arnold at the time he went on with reinforcements to the relief of the garrisson at Fort Stanwix. He was also a volunteer under Gov. Geo. Clinton at the time he went north to intercept the retreat of sir John Johnson, and was one of the two scouts, who were selected by the governor, and sent from Crown Point, to scour the wilderness between that post and Schroon lake; and also performed many other similar, important and hazardous duties, an account of which is now on record. He was also with the American army from the time of its retreat from Fort Edward to Van Schaick's island, except when otherwise employed, and on its return to Bemis's Heights, assisting with his team in conveying the baggage of the army. He also remained with the army during its whole stay on Bemis's Heights, and until the time of Burgoyne's surrender at Saratoga, and became familiarly acquainted with all the officers, and actually led out, or piloted three regiments to the field of action—the country then being principally a wilderness, and executed many other important duties. He also continued to live at the same place until the time of his decease in '33, and on the very ground and in its vicinity where those important battles and interesting movements of the two contending armies, of which the author is about to write, took place, and consequently, the reader, he thinks, as well as the author himself, will say that he must of course, and beyond the possibility of doubt, have been familiarly acquainted with every portion of the ground on which every action was fought, and with the movements of each and every brigade, regiment, and batallion of the two contending armies, and especially of the American.

In addition to the foregoing, the author will add, that, he being a man of well known ability to communicate, and of strong and retentive memory, even of the most minute circumstances, it is, therefore, more than probable, that he retained as far as it was possible for frail man to retain, a full, clear, and comprehensive recollection of all the facts and circumstances, which the author is about to disclose, until they were communicated and often repeated to and treasured up by him, in all their simplicity and truth, and who now as a most faithful and humble servant presents them before a generous and charitable public.

The author is well aware of his responsibility in as much as his own account in many instances, will differ very materially from the most, if not all of those who have written upon the subject. Not that he would mean to be understood to say, that all others are intentionally in an error; but on the contrary, when he looks at the materials out of which their superstructures have been erected, he feels more charitably disposed towards them than he otherwise would feel, had their premises been true from which they have drawn their false conclusions. It has been frequently remarked, that in the original accounts given of the several movements of the two armies, and especially of the battles fought between them, there are no two who agree in their statements. This is a lamentable fact, and having been well weighed in the author's mind, more strongly confirms him if possible in the authenticity of the account which he has received from those who had, and continued to have, the best possible means of observing and retaining the facts as they transpired. The reader will bear in mind, that the time when those original accounts were written by the officers, or others connected with the armies, was a time of much confusion and alarm, and a time of the greatest excitement; when the minds of the people generally, were on the utmost stretch, to catch at something favorable on the one side, or unfavorable on the other; and consequently under such circumstances, and during the moment of such excitement, it is not be be wondered at, that all the accounts then hastily drawn up, and hurriedly despatched to some general officer, or particular friend, should be wanting in many prominent particulars, and redundant in others. Gen. Washington himself often complained of the many different and conflicting statements which came to him, and which seemed at the time to baffle all conjecture. And the author would now ask the reader to place his finger on one single sentence, which he can select from those original accounts, that has been altered or corrected by its author; and if he is not able to do that, he would again ask, to which *one* of them, for they are numerous, will he give his assent, and reject all others as incorrect.

In giving an account of some of the numerous incidents connected with Burgoyne's Campaign, the author will do it in as few words as possible, and retain the substance of the facts as they transpired.

As this is the author's first and only attempt at "book-making," and as he is duly sensible of the delicate situation in which he has very reluctantly placed himself—though his aim is sincerely to do good, by recording what he verily believes to be a plain and simple state-of facts; he earnestly hopes, therefore, that all his imperfections either in style or arrangement, will be indulgently overlooked by the reader, of whom he will, for the present, take his leave with the following motto—

"Truth ought always to be preferred before elegance of language."

THE AUTHOR.

PREFACE.

The final move to perpetuate the Saratoga Battlefield was started in Troy Rotary in July last year, at which time it was decided to interest clubs in this section in a celebration on September 19th. Invitations were sent to all Rotary clubs in this vicinity and in Western Massachusetts and Vermont. Personal appeals were also made to Rotary to attend.

Invitations were sent to President Coolidge and the governors of Massachusetts, Vermont and New York State, the Attorney-General of the U. S., Senators Copeland, Wadsworth, Congressman Parker, Senator Brown, Assemblyman Esmond, Mr. White of Utica, Mr. Ogden of Rochester, Mr. Ochs of the New York *Times*. The President sent regrets as did the governors, and the Attorney-General and U. S. Senators, but Congressman Parker, Mr. Ochs, Senator Brown, Assemblyman Esmond, Mayor Gilmor of Utica, Mayor Martin of Rome, several councilmen and aldermen of these two cities, Mr. W. Pierpont White, Mr. Charles E. Ogden,

Mr. Louis King, President of the Mohawk Valley Association were there and the celebration was a decided success. It was a wonderful day. The Mothers Club of Bemis Heights handled about 400 at the luncheon at the historic Neilson farm, where Mr. Ogden made a stirring address for the preservation of the Battlefields. The meeting adjourned to the Sanders farm, which was donated by Mr. John Sanders for the balance of the afternoon and speeches were made by Mr. White, Congressman Parker, Mr. King, Mr. Esmond and Mr. Ochs. The Rotary committee which consisted of George O. Slingerland as chairman and Robert W. Fisher secretary, with members of the Troy, Albany, Glens Falls, Granville, Saratoga, Amsterdam, Hudson Falls and Cobleskill clubs, was continued to further the idea of rousing public interest in this great undertaking.

Just after this celebration, I started to feel out public interest by personal talks before different bodies, by writing and by sending out a form of endorsement to be filled out by the bodies addressed. The response was wonderful. The Masonic Bodies, the K. of C. Bodies, Fire Departments, City Councils, Boards of Aldermen, Churches Societies, Mother's Clubs,

PREFACE xvii

Banks, Travelling Men's Associations, Elks, Foresters, V. of F. W., Legions, DeMolay, Sons of Revolution, Daughters of Revolution, Educational Associations, Patriotic Dames, Ancient and Honorable Artillery Company of Boston, DeMolay of San Diego, Cal. The interest taken by all who were asked to pass resolutions was very great and in January, Mr. Esmond, Assemblyman from Saratoga County, introduced a bill that, after being cut down in regard to the appropriation and changed around a lot, was passed by both houses, Friday, the 23rd of April. The bill was signed by the Governor on May 10th, 1926.

In 1844, Charles Neilson, the grandfather of the present occupant, in his history of the Burgoyne Campaign, deplores the fact that the State or Nation had never done anything to preserve the battlefield.

In 1877 at the one hundredth anniversary of the battle and dedication of the Schuylerville monument, the fact was deplored that nothing had ever been done in 100 years by State or Nation. Historical societies and members of families had placed stones here and there on the field and no real move was made until 1923, when the Saratoga Battlefield Association took title to the Freeman and Sarles farms, as a holding company for the State or Nation. This was the real start in a practical way. Then the celebration by the Rotary Clubs was the second step. Then the support of Mr. Ochs of the New York *Times,* Mr. Hutton of the *Knickerbocker Press,* Mr. Walbridge of the *Saratogian,* Mr. Marvin of the Troy *Record,* Mr. Williams of the Utica *Daily Press,* the Glens Falls *Star,* Troy *Times,* Mechanicville *Times,* Cohoes *American,* New York *World,* Rochester *Herald* and a great many other newspapers who devoted a great deal of space to the Battlefield Idea, made the next step toward the result. The Esmond bill, the hearing before the Ways and Means Committee, then the conference with the Governor at which apparently all doubts were removed, then came some other misunderstandings that about stopped the progress of the bill through the houses, but finally the Senate and Assembly concurred and the bill was finally passed. The Conservation Commission and Educational Department are entitled to a large share of applause for their work in making this dream of 150 years a realization. Perhaps the outstanding figures working for the great achievement are the names of Mr. Ochs, Mr. Hutton, Mr.

Esmond, Dr. Flick, Mr. Ogden and the patriotic land-owners who made it possible to get the land at a reasonable figure, Mr. Charles Neilson and family, Mr. James Cannon and family, Mrs. Sarle and Mrs. Jennie Wright. In fact all societies, newspapers and individuals should have a just share of commendation for the good work in doing a patriotic duty to perpetuate the memory of the ragged, untrained, continentals, farmers, woodsmen, who stopped the invaders at Bemis Heights and who made it possible for this great Nation to be.

What of the future? The whole area of the occupancy of the British and American forces should be acquired. The road leading from the Freeman road along the river suitably marked, the lands adjacent to Fish Creek at Schuylerville, the Birkett property, where the British army forded the Hudson, the heights at Victory, the Schuyler Mansion, Marshall house, Dovegat house, Freeman house, Powder Magazine on the Neilson farm, General Gates' headquarters, (American and British headquarters rebuilt) the embankments, breast works and redoubts occupied by Morgan, Poor, Arnold, Burgoyne restored and then all states whose soldiers took part in the battle should erect monuments at different points over the battlefield. The wooded sections and the clearings reproduced, good roads to wind about the whole field so that the student and patriot worshipper could trail each act of those thirty or more days that decided the fate of the Nation. Suitable parking places provided where one could sit and not only enjoy the wonderful beauties that Nature provided for a background, but could trace step by step and hour by hour, the waging of the battles.

Families of those who fought for our liberty should come forward with appropriate markers or monuments so the future citizens should know the names of those who helped make the Nation. The plot of land west of the Neilson residence should be made a hallowed spot by the State of New York, for there it is understood, the bones of those who died, have helped enrich the soil. A wonderful, beautiful cemetery could be made there.

One section of the battlefield should be made into a landing place for aeroplanes, looking to the future to provide a means of travel by air. And appropriate signs and markers provided everywhere so the tourist, student and patriot can know where each incident of the battles that is known can be pointed out.

The central office of the whole park should be a dignified colonial structure that would house the only building left on the battlefield at this date, 1926, and provide a museum of interesting early Americana and relics of this battlefield and surrounding country, a tool house and water supply arranged for, roads and foot paths winding through stately trees that will be under the care and protection of the conservation commission.

The wonderful natural setting of Bemis Heights with the lordly Hudson and foot hills of the Green Mountains of Vermont eastward and the Bennington battle ground almost in sight, should make this the most patriotic and scenic park in the whole Nation.

GEORGE O. SLINGERLAND.

MECHANICVILLE, N. Y., *June* 10, 1926.

BURGOYNE'S CAMPAIGN.

CHAPTER I

During the progress of the Revolutionary War, the British minister formed the scheme of opening a way to New-York, by means of an army which should descend from Lake Champlain to the banks of the Hudson, and unite in the vicinity of Albany with the whole, or with a part of that commanded by Gen. Howe. All intercourse would then have been cut off between the Eastern and Western provinces, and it was believed that victory from that moment, could no longer be doubtful. This expedition to them, presented few difficulties, since, with the exception of a short march, it might be executed entirely by water. It was hoped that it would have been already effected by the close of the preceding year; but it had failed in consequence of the obstacles encountered upon the lakes, the lateness of the season, and especially because while Gen. Carlton, then Governor of Canada, advanced upon Ticonderoga, and consequently towards the Hudson, Gen. Howe, instead of proceeding up the river to join him, had carried his arms against New Jersey. At present, however, this scheme had acquired new favor, and what in the preceding years had been only an incidental part of the plan of the campaign, was now become its main object. The entire British nation had founded the most sanguine expectations upon this arrangement; nothing else seemed to be talked of among them but this expedition of Canada, which was shortly to bring about the total subjection of America. The junction of the two armies appeared quite sufficient to attain this desired object; the Americans, it was said, could not oppose it without coming to a general battle, and in such case, there could exist no doubt of the result. The ministers had taken all the measures which they deemed essential to the success of so important an enterprise; they had furnished with profusion whatever the generals themselves had required or suggested.

General Burgoyne, an officer of uncontested

ability, possessed of an exact knowledge of the country, and animated by an ardent thirst for military glory, had repaired to England during the preceeding winter, where he had submitted to the ministers the plan of this expedition, and had concerted with them the means of carrying it into effect. The ministry, besides their confidence in his genius and spirit, placed great hope in that eager desire of renown by which they knew him to be goaded incessantly; they gave him therefore the direction of all the operations.

General Burgoyne arrived in Quebec in the beginning of the month of May 1777, and immediately set himself to push forward the business of his mission. He displayed an extreme activity in completing all the preparations which might conduce to the success of the enterprise. Meanwhile, several ships arrived from England, bringing arms, munitions, and field equipage, in great abundance; and every thing was in preparation for an expedition which was to decide the event of the war, and the fate of America.

The regular force placed at the disposal of Burgoyne, consisting of British and German troops, amounted to upwards of seven thousand men, exclusive of a corps of artillery composed of about five hundred. To these were added a detachment of seven hundred rangers, under Col. St. Ledger, destined to make an excursion into the Mohawk country, and to seize Fort Stanwix, otherwise called Fort Schuyler. This corps consisted of some companies of English infantry, of recruits from New-York, Hanau chasseurs, and of a party of Canadians and savages. He was also joined by about two thousand Canadians including axemen, and other workmen, who services, it was foreseen, would be much needed to render the ways practicable. A sufficient number of seamen had been assembled for manning the transports upon the lakes and upon the Hudson. Besides the Canadians that were to be immediately attached to the army, many others were called upon to scour the wood in the frontiers, and to occupy the intermediate posts between the army which advanced towards the Hudson, and that which remained for the protection of Canada; the latter amounted, including the Highland emigrants to upwards of three thousand men. In addition to the foregoing, a host of savages from their avidity to grasp the presents of the

English or from their innate thirst for blood and plunder, were induced to join the British army. Never, perhaps, was an army of no greater force than this accompanied by so formidable a train of artillery, as well from the number of pieces as from the skill of those who served it. This powerful apparatus was considered eminently sufficient to disperse without effort an undisciplined enemy in the open country, or to dislodge him from any difficult places. The generals who seconded Burgoyne in this expedition were all able and excellent officers. The principal were major-general Philips, of the artillery, who had distinguished himself in the wars of Germany, the brigadier-generals Frazer, Powall and Hamilton, with the Brunswick major-general baron Reidesel, and brigader-generals Specht and Goll. The whole army shared in the ardor and hopes of its chiefs, not a doubt was entertained of an approaching triumph, and the conquest of America. The preparations being at length completed, and all the troops, as well national as auxiliary, having arrived, Burgoyne proceeded to encamp near the little river Bouquet, in now Essex county, upon the west bank of Lake Champlain, at no great distance to the north of Crown Point. As the time for commencing hostilities was near at hand and dreading the consequences of the barbarity of the savages, which, besides the dishonor it reflected on the British arms, might prove essentially prejudicial to the success of the expedition, he made a speech to them, calculated, in terms of singular energy, to excite their ardor in the common cause, and at the same time to repress their ferocious propensities.

While on the one hand general Burgoyne attempted to mitigate the natural ferocity of the Indians, he endeavored on the other, to render them an object of terror with those who persisted in resistance. For this purpose, on the twenty-ninth of June, he issued a general proclamation from his camp at Putnam Creek, wherein he magnified the force of the British armies and fleets which were about to embrace and to crush every part of America. He had come, he continued, with a numerous and veteran army, to put an end to the enormities of the people. He invited the well-disposed to join him, and assist in redeeming their country from slavery, and in the re-establishment of legal government. He promised protection and security to all those who should continue quietly to pursue their occupations; who should abstain from removing their cattle or corn, or any species of forage; from breaking up the bridges, or obstructing the roads, and in a word, from committing any act of hostilities; and who, on the contrary, should furnish the camp with all sorts of provisions, assured, as they might be, of receiving the full value thereof in solid coin. But against the contumacious, and those who should persist in rebellion, he denounced the most terrible war; he warned them that justice and vengeance were about to overtake them accompanied with devastation, famine, and all the calamities of war in their train. Finally, he admonished them not to flatter themselves, that distance or coverts could screen them from his pursuit, for he had only to let loose the thousands of Indians that were under his direction, to discover in their most secret retreats, and to punish with condign severity the hardened enemies of Great Britain.

That fearless people who inhibited the provinces, and especially New England, far from allowing this manifesto to terrify them, were much inclined to deride it; they never met with each other without contemptuously enquiring what vent the vaunting general of *Britain* had found for his pompous and ridiculous declamations.

These preliminary dispositions accomplished, Burgoyne made a short stop at Crown Point, for the establishment of magazines, an hospital, and other necessary services, and then proceeded with all his troops to invest Ticonderoga. From Crown Point, the British army advanced on both sides of the lake, the naval force keeping its station in the center; the frigate and gun boats cast anchor just out of cannon shot from the American works. On the near approach of the right wing, which advanced on the west side of the lake, on the second of July, the Americans abandoned and set fire to their works, block-houses and sawmills, towards lake George; and without attempting any serious opposition, suffered Gen. Phillips to take possession of Mount Hope. This post commanded the American lines in a great degree, and cut off their communication with Lake George. The enemy charged the Americans, on this occasion, with supineness and want of vigor; but this charge seems not well founded: they had not men enough to make any effectual opposition to the powerful force which threatened to enclose them.

In the meantime, the British army proceeded with such expedition in the construction of their works, the bringing up of their artillery, stores, and provisions, and the establishment of posts and communications, that by the fifth matters were so far advanced as to require but one or two days to completely invest the posts on both sides of the lake. Mount Defiance had also been examined, and the advantages which it presented were so important, that it had been determined to take possession and erect a battery there. This work, though attended with extreme difficulty and labor, had been carried on by Gen. Phillips with much expedition and success. A road had been made over very rough ground, to the top of the mound; and the enemy were at work in constructing a level for a battery and transporting their cannon. As soon as this battery should be ready to play, the American works would have been completely invested on all sides.

The situation of Gen. St. Clair, who was in command of the Fort at Ticonderoga, was now very critical. He called a council of war to deliberate on measures to be taken. He informed them that their whole effective number was not sufficient to man one-half of the works; that as the whole must be constantly on duty, it would be impossible for them to endure the fatigue for any considerable length of time; that Gen. Schuyler, who was then at Fort Edward, had not sufficient forces to relieve them; and that as the enemy's batteries were nearly ready to open upon them, and the place would be completely invested in twenty-four hours, nothing could save the troops but an immediate evacuation of the posts.

It was proposed that the baggage of the army, with such artillery, stores and provisions as the necessity of the occasion would admit, should be embarked with a strong detachment on board of two hundred batteaux, and despatched under convoy of five armed galleys, up the lake to Skeensborough (Whitehall,) and that the main body of the army should proceed by land, taking its route on the road to Castleton in Vermont, which was about thirty miles south-east of Ticonderoga, and join the boats and galleys at Skeensborough. It was thought necessary to keep the matter a secret till the time should come when it was to be executed. Hence the necessary preparations could not be made, and it was not possible to prevent irregularity and disorder in the differet embarcations and movements of the troops. About two o'clock in the morning of July 6th, Gen. St. Clair left Ticonderoga, and about three, the troops at Mount Independence were put in motion. The house which had been occupied by Gen. de Fermoy was, contrary to orders, set on fire. This afforded complete information to the enemy of what was going forward, and enabled them to see every movement of the Americans; at the same time it impressed the latter with such an idea of discovery and danger, as precipitated them into great disorder.

About four o'clock Colonel Francis brought off the rear-guard, and conducted their retreat in a regular manner, and soon after, some of the regiments, through the exertions of their officers, recovered from their confusion. When the troops arrived at Hubbardton, in Vermont, they were halted for nearly two hours, and the rear-guard was increased by many who did not at first belong to it, but were picked up on the road, having been unable to keep up with their regiments. The rear-guard was here put under the command of Col. Seth Warner, with orders to follow the army, as soon as the whole camp came up, and to halt a mile and a half short of the main body. The army then proceeded to Castleton, about six miles farther—Col. Warner, with the rear-guard and stragglers, remaining at Hubbardton.

The retreat of the Americans from Ticonderoga and Mount Independence, was no sooner perceived by the British, than Gen. Frazer began an eager pursuit with his brigade. Major-General Reidesel was ordered to join in the pursuit with the greater part of his Germans. General Frazer continued the pursuit through the day, and having received intelligence that the rear-guard of the American army was at no great distance, ordered his men to lie that night upon their arms. On the 7th July, at five o'clock in the morning, he came up with Colonel Warner, who had about one thousand men. The British advanced boldly to the attack, and the two bodies formed within sixty yards of each other. The conflict was fierce and bloody. Colonel Francis fell at the head of his regiment, fighting with great gallantry. Colonel Warner was so well supported by his officers and men, that the assailants broke and gave way. They soon, however, recovered from their disorder, formed again, and charged the Americans with the bayonet, when they, in their turn, were put into disorder; these however rallied and returned to the charge, and the issue of the battle became dubious. At that moment General Reidesel appeared with the advanced party of his Germans. These being led into action, soon decided the fortune of the day, and the Americans had to retreat. The loss in this action was very considerable on the American side. Col. Hale, who had not brought his regiment, which consisted of militia, into action, although ordered so to do, in attempting to escape by flight, fell in with an inconsiderable party of the enemy, and surrendered himself, and a number of his men, prisoners. In killed, wounded and prisoners, the Americans lost in this action three hundred and twenty-four men, and the British one hundred and eighty-three in killed and wounded.

Burgoyne having determined to pursue the Americans by water, the British seamen and artificers immediately engaged in the operation of destroying the boom and bridge which had been constructed in front of Fort Ti or Ticonderoga. The passage being cleared, the ships of Burgoyne immediately entered Wood Creek and proceeded with extreme rapidity in search of the Americans, who had taken that route; all was in motion at once upon land and water.

By three in the afternoon, the van of the British squadron, composed of gun boats, came up with and attacked the American galleys, near Skeenesborough. In the meantime three regiments, which had been landed at South Bay, ascended and passed a mountain with great expedition, in order to turn the Americans above Wood Creek, to destroy their works at Skeenesborough, and thus to cut off their retreat to Fort Ann. But the Americans eluded this stroke by the rapidity of their flight. The British frigates having joined the van, the galleys already hard pushed by the gun boats, were completely overpowered. Two of them surrendered; three were blown up. The Americans now despaired; having set fire to their works, mills, and batteaux, and otherwise destroyed what they were unable to burn, they escaped as well as they could up Wood Creek, without halting till they reached Fort Ann. Their loss was considerable, for the batteaux they burnt were loaded with baggage, provisions, and munitions, as necessary to their sustenance as to military operations.

General St. Clair, who had arrived with the van-guard at Castleton, in Vermont, upon intelligence of the discomfiture at Hubbardton, and the disaster of Skeenesborough, which was brought to him at the same time by an officer of one of the galleys, apprehensive that he should be interrupted if he proceeded towards Fort Ann, struck into the woods on the left, uncertain whether he should repair to New England, or to Fort Edward. But being joined two days after, at Manchester, by the remains of the corps of Colonel Warner, and having collected the fugitives, he proceeded to Fort Edward, in order to unite with General Schuyler.

After the surrender of Fort Ticonderoga, General Burgoyne endeavored to keep up the alarm, by spreading his parties over the country. With this view, Colonel Hill, at the head of the ninth regiment, was despatched after Colonel Long, who with four or five hundred men, principally invalids and convalescents of the army, had taken post at Fort Ann, and was directed by General Schuyler to defend it. Colonel Long with his party did not wait an attack from the enemy, but boldly advanced to meet them.

At half past ten in the morning he attacked the British in front, with a heavy and well directed fire; a large body passed the creek on the left, and fired from a thick wood across the creek on the left flank of the regiment: they then began to recross the creek and attack the enemy in the rear. Colonel Hill then found it necessary to change his ground, to prevent his regiment from being surrounded. He took post upon the top of a hill to his right. As soon as he had taken post, the Americans made a very vigorous attack, which continued for upwards of two hours, and they would have certainly forced the enemy, had it not been for some Indians that arrived, and gave the Indian war-whoop, which was answered by the enemy with three cheers. The Americans soon after that gave way. The giving way of the Americans was caused not, however, by the terror of the war whoop, but by the failure of their ammunition. The following is a very correct description of the scene of this action.

On leaving the street of Fort Ann village,

there is a bridge over Wood Creek, leading to its left bank. Immediately beyond the bridge there is a narrow pass, only wide enough for a carriage, and cut, in a great measure, out of a rocky ledge, which terminates here exactly at the creek. This ledge is the southern end of a high rocky hill, which converges towards Wood Creek, and between the two is a narrow tract of level ground, which terminates at the pass already mentioned. On this ground the battle took place, and the wood on the right bank of the creek, from which the Americans fired upon the left flank of the British, is still there, and it was up this rocky hill that they retreated and took their stand.

General Burgoyne, as usual, claimed a victory in this affair, which is understood to have been a bloody contest, as indeed it obviously must have been from the narrowness of the defile, and the consequent nearness of the contending parties. Captain Montgomery, of Colonel Hill's regiment, was left wounded on the field, and taken prisoner by the Americans, which could not have been the fact, had the royal party been victorious.

Colonel Long, deeming it not prudent to remain longer at Fort Ann, as the main body of the British army was on its near approach, set fire to the fort, and withdrew with his Spartan band to Fort Edward.

After the arrival of General St. Clair at Fort Edward on the twelfth, and of the fugitives, who came in by companies, all the American troops amounted to a little over four thousand men, including militia. They were in want of all necessaries, and even of courage, in consequence of their reverses. The Americans lost in these different actions no less than one hundred and twenty-eight pieces of artillery, with a prodigious quantity of warlike stores, baggage and provisions, particularly of flour, which they left in Ticonderoga and Mount Independence. To increase the calamity, the whole of the neighboring country was struck with terror by this torrent of disasters, and the inhabitants thought more of providing for their own safety, than of flying to the succor of their country in jeopardy. The country between Fort Ann and Fort Edward, a distance of about sixteen miles, was extremely rough and savage; the ground unequal, and broken with numerous streams, and with wide and deep morasses. General Schuyler neglected no means of adding by art to the difficulties

with which nature seemed to have purposely
interdicted this passage. Trenches were opened,
the roads and paths obstructed, the bridges
broken up; and in the only practicable defiles
immense trees were cut in such a manner on
both sides, of the road, as to fall across and
lengthwise, which with their branches inter-
woven, presented an insurmountable barrier;
in a word, this wilderness, in itself so horrible,
was thus rendered almost absolutely impene-
trable. He also directed the cattle to be removed to the most distant places, and the
stores and baggage from Fort George to Fort
Edward, that articles of such necessity for his
troops might not fall into the hands of the
enemy. He urgently demanded that all the
regiments of regular troops found in the adjacent provinces, should be sent without delay
to join him; he also made earnest calls upon
the militia of New England and New York.

While he thus occupied himself with so
much ardor, General Burgoyne was detained
at Skeenesborough as well by the difficulty
of the ground he had to pass, as because
he had to wait for the arrival of tents, baggage, artillery and provisions, so absolutely
necessary before plunging himself into these

fearful solitudes. His army at this time was disposed in the following manner: the right occupied the heights of Skeenesborough, the German division of Reidesel forming its extremity; the left, composed of Brunswickers, extending into the plain, rested upon the river at Castleton, and the brigade of Frazer formed the centre. The regiment of Hessians of Hanau was posted at the source of East Creek, to protect the camp of Castleton and the batteaux upon Wood Creek, against the incursions of Warner, who had been detached with his regiment into the state of Vermont, with orders to assemble the militia of the country, and to make incursions towards Ticonderoga. In the meantime, indefatigable labor was exerted in removing all obstacles to the navigation of Wood Creek, and also in clearing passages and opening roads through the country about Fort Ann. The design of Burgoyne was, that the main body of the army should penetrate through the wilderness we have just described to Fort Edward, while another column under General Phillips embarking at Ticonderoga, should proceed up Lake George, reduce the fort of that name situated at its southern extremity, and afterwards rejoin him at Fort Edward. Upon the acquisition of Fort George, the stores, provisions and necessaries were to be conveyed to the camp by way of the lake, the navigation of which was easier and more expeditious than that of Wood Creek, and there was, besides, a good wagon road between the two posts. Such were the efforts made by the two belligerents; the English believing themselves secure of victory; the Americans hardly venturing to hope for better fortune.

CHAPTER II

In the meantime, Colonel St. Leger, whose detachment had been reinforced by a large body of Indians under Brant, (alias Tayadanaga) the great captain of the Six Nations, went up the St. Lawrence, then to Oswego, and from thence to Fort Stanwix. From this point it was intended to pass down the Mohawk and join the forces of Burgoyne at Albany. In June '76, general Schuyler, who had the command of the north western frontier, sent Colonel Dayton to repair the works at Fort Stanwix:

he seems to have done little towards effecting this object; he however, thought proper to change its name to Fort Schuyler, which name it retained during the war. The last of April '77, Colonel Peter Gansevoort with the third regiment of the New-York line of troops, was sent to supply his place.

Fort Stanwix, which stood on the present site of the village of Rome in Oneida county, and named from General Stanwix, was originally erected in the year 1758, during the French war. It occupied a position commanding the carrying place between the navigable waters of the Mohawk and Wood Creek, and was regarded as the key to the communication between Canada and the settlements on the Mohawk. It was originally a square fort, having four bastions surmounting a broad and deep ditch, with a covert way and glacis. In the centre of the ditch, a row of perpendicular pickets was planted, and another horizontal row fixed around the ramparts. But although the principal fortress had been erected at the enormous expense for those times of $266,400, yet at the commencement of the revolutionary war the whole was in ruins.

On the third of August, Colonel St. Leger

arrived before the fort with his whole force, consisting of a motly collection of British regulars, Hessians, Tories, and about one thousand Indians. The garrison under Col. Gansevoort, consisted of about seven hundred and fifty men. Soon after his arrival, St. Leger sent a flag into the fort with a manifesto, advising submission to the mercy of the king, and denouncing severe vengeance against those who should continue in their unnatural rebellion. This manifesto produced no effect on the brave garrison, who had determined to defend the fortress to the last extremity. Apprised of this state of things, and knowing the importance of this post to the United States, General Herkimer summoned the militia of Tryon county to the field to march to the succor of the garrison. On the fifth of August he arrived near Oriskany with a body of upwards of 800 men, all eager to meet the enemy. On the morning of the sixth, General Herkimer determined to halt till he had received reinforcements, or at least until the signal of a sortie should be received from the fort. His officers, however, were eager to press forward; high words ensued, during which the two colonels and other officers denounced their commander to his face, as a tory and a coward. The brave old man calmly replied that he considered himself placed over them as a father, and that it was not his wish to lead them into any difficulty from which he could not extricate them. Burning, as they now seemed, to meet the enemy, he told them roundly that they would run at his first appearance, but his remonstrances were unavailing. Their clamor increased, and their reproaches were repeated, until, stung by imputations of cowardice and want of fidelity to the cause, and somewhat irritated withal, the general immediately gave the order—" march on! " The words were no sooner heard than the troops gave a shout, and moved, or rather rushed forward. Colonel St. Leger having heard of the advance of general Herkimer, determined to attack him in an ambuscade. The spot chosen favored the design. There was a deep ravine crossing the path which Herkimer was traversing, sweeping towards the east in a semi-circular form, and bearing in a northern and southern direction. The bottom of this ravine was marshy, and the road crossed it by means of a causeway. The ground, thus partly enclosed by the ravine, was elevated and level. The ambuscade was laid upon the high ground west of the ravine.

The British troops, with a large body of Indians under Brant disposed themselves in a circle, leaving only a narrow segment open for the admission of Herkimer's troops. Unconscious of the presence of the enemy, Gen. Herkimer with his whole force, with the exception of the rear guard, found themselves encompassed at the onset—the foe closing up the gap on their first fire. Those on the outside fled as their commander had predicted; those within the circle were thrown into disorder by the sudden and murderous fire now poured in upon them on all sides. General Herkimer fell wounded in the early part of the action, and was placed on his saddle against the trunk of a tree for his support, and thus continued to order the battle. The action having lasted more than half an hour in great disorder, Herkimer's men formed themselves into circles to repel the attacks of the enemy, who were now closing in upon them from all sides. From this moment their resistance was more effective. The firing in a great measure ceased; and the conflict was carried on with knives, bayonets, and the butt-ends of their muskets. A heavy shower of rain now arrested the work of death; the storm raged for an hour, and the enemy retired among the trees, at a respectful distance, having suffered severely, notwithstanding the advantages in their favor. During this suspension of the conflict, General Herkimer's men, by his direction, formed themselves into a circle and awaited the movements of the enemy. In the early part of the battle, whenever a gun was fired by a militiaman from behind a tree, an Indian rushed up and tomahawked him before he could reload. To counteract this, two men were stationed behind a single tree, one only to fire at a time—the other to reserve his fire, till the Indian ran up as before. The fight was soon renewed, but by this arrangement the Indians suffered so severely that they began to give way. A reinforcement of the enemy now came up, called Johnson's Greens. These men were mostly royalists, who, having fled from Tryon county, now returned in arms against their former neighbors. Many of the militia and Greens knew each other, and as soon as they advanced near enough for recognition, mutual feelings of hate and revenge raged in their bosoms. The militia fired upon them as they advanced, and then springing like tigers from their coverts, attacked them with their bayonets and butts of their muskets; or both parties in close contest throttled each other and drew their knives—stabbing and sometimes literally dying in each other's embrace.

This murderous conflict did not continue long: the Indians seeing with what resolution the militia continued the fight, and finding their own numbers greatly diminished, now raised the retreating cry *"Oonah!"* and fled in every direction under the shouts of the surviving militia, and a shower of bullets. A firing was heard in the distance, from the fort; the Greens and Rangers now deemed that their presence was necessary elsewhere, and retreated precipitately, leaving the victorious militia of Tryon county masters of the field. Thus ended one of the severest, and for the numbers engaged, one of the most bloody battles of the revolutionary war.

The loss of the militia, according to the American account, was two hundred killed, exclusive of wounded and prisoners. The loss of the enemy was equally if not more severe, than that of the Americans. General

Herkimer, though wounded in the onset, bore himself during the six hours of conflict under the most trying circumstances, with a degree of fortitude and composure worthy of admiration. At one time during the battle, while sitting upon his saddle, raised upon a little hillock, being advised to select a less exposed situation, he replied, "I will face the enemy." Thus surrounded by a few men, he continued to issue his orders with firmness. In this situation, and in the midst of the onslaught, he deliberately took his tinder box from his pocket, lit his pipe, and smoked with great composure. After the battle was over he was removed from the field on a litter and conveyed to his house, below the Little Falls on the Mohawk.

At the time of the battle of Oriskany, when general Herkimer was advancing to the relief of the fort, a diversion was made in his favor, by a sortie of two hundred and fifty men under the command of Colonel Willet. Such was the impetuosity of Willet's movements, that sir John Johnson and his regiment, who law near the fort with his Indian allies, sought safty in flight. The amount of spoil found in the enemy's camp was so great that Willet sent hastily for wagons to convey it away. The spoil thus captured, twenty wagon loads, consisted of camp equipage, clothing, blankets, stores, &c., five British standards, and the baggage and papers of most of the officers. For this brilliant exploit, congress directed that Colonel Willet should be presented with an elegant sword in the name of the United States.

The siege of the fort still continued, and the situation of the garrison, though not desperate, began to be somewhat critical. Colonel Willet and Major Stockwell readily undertook the hazardous mission of passing through the enemy's lines to arouse their countrymen to their relief. After creeping on their hands and knees through the enemy's encampment, and adopting various arts of concealment, they pursued their way through swampy and pathless woods until they arrived safely at German Flats, and from thence to the head quarters of General Schuyler, then commanding the American army at Stillwater.

General Arnold was immediately despatched with a body of regular troops and volunteer militia raised for the occasion, to the relief of Col. Gansevoort. As he was advancing up the

Mohawk, he captured a tory by the name of Hon Yost Schuyler, who being a spy was condemned to death. Hon Yost was one of the coarsest and most ignorant men in the valley, appearing scarcely half removed from idiocy; and yet there was no small share of shrewdness in his character. He was promised his life if he would go to the enemy, particularly the Indians, and alarm them by announcing that a large army of the Americans was in full march to destroy them. Hon Yost being acquainted with many of the Indians, gladly accepted the offer; one of his brothers was detained as a hostage for his fidelity, and was to be hung if he proved treacherous. A friendly Oneida Indian was let into the secret, and cheerfully embarked in the design. Upon Hon Yost's arrival he told a lamentable story of his being taken by Arnold, and of his escape from being hanged; he showed them several shot holes in his coat, which he said were made by bullets fired at him when making his escape. Knowing the character of the Indians, he communicated his intelligence to them in a mysterious and imposing manner. When asked the number of men which Arnold had, he shook his head mysteriously, and pointed upwards towards the leaves of the trees. These reports spread rapidly through the camp. Meantime the friendly Oneida arrived with a belt and confirmed what Hon Yost had said, hinting that a bird had brought him intelligence of great moment. On his way to the camp of the beseigers he had fallen in with two or three Indians of his acquaintance, who readily engaged in furthering his design.— These sagacious fellows dropped into the camp as if by accident, they spoke of warriors in great numbers rapidly advancing against them. The Americans, it was stated did not wish to injure the Indians, but if they continued with the British they must all share one common fate. The Indians were thoroughly alarmed, and determined on an immediate flight, being already disgusted with the British service. Colonel St. Leger exhorted, argued and made enticing offers to the Indians to remain, but all in vain. He attempted to get them drunk, but they refused to drink. When he determined to go, he urged them to move in the rear of his army; but they charged him with a design to sacrifice them to his safety. In a mixture of rage and despair, he broke up his encampment with such haste, that he left his tents, cannon and stores to the besiegers. The friendly Oneida accompanied the flying army, and being naturally a wag, he engaged his companions, who were in the secret, to repeat at proper intervals the cry—*"They are coming!" "They are coming!"* This appaling cry quickened the flight of the fugitives whenever it was heard. The soldiers threw away their packs; and the commanders took care not to be in the rear. After much fatigue and mortification, they finally reached Oneida Lake, and there probably for the first time felt secure from the pursuit of their enemies. From this place St. Leger hastened with his scattered forces back to Oswego and thence to Montreal.

Hon Yost, after accompanying the flying army as far as the estuary of Wood Creek, left them and retired to Fort Schuyler, (Stanwix,) and gave the first information to Colonel Gansevoort of the approach of Arnold. From thence he proceeded to German Flats, and on presenting himself at Fort Dayton his brother was discharged. He soon after rejoined the British standard, attaching himself to the forces under Sir John Johnson.

Arnold, having quitted the main body, and

with a light armed detachment of only nine hundred men, set forward by forced marches towards the fortress, and arrived at the fort on the evening of the twenty-fourth of August, two days after the siege had been raised. He and his soldiers were welcomed by the garrison with acknowledgements of deliverance, and the exultation of victory.

The following incident, which took place near Oriskany, may be interesting to the reader, as showing the unlimited confidence which might, in those days, be placed in the Indians, when pledged to perform any certain act within their power.

An old Indian named Han-Yerry, who during the war had acted with the royal party, and now resided at Oriskany in a log wigwam which stood on the bank of the creek, just back of the house until recently occupied by Mr. Charles Green, one day called at Judge White's with his wife and a mulatto woman who belonged to him, and who acted as his interpreter. After conversing with him a little while, the Indian asked him,

"Are you my friend?"

"Yes," said he.

"Well, then," said the Indian, "do you believe I am your friend?"

"Yes, Han-Yerry," replied he, "I believe you are."

The Indian then rejoined, "Well, if you are my friend, and you believe I am your friend, I will tell you what I want, and then I shall know whether you speak true words."

"And what is that you want?" said Mr. White.

The Indian pointed to a little grandchild, the daughter of one of his sons, then between two and three years old, and said,

"My squaw wants to take this pappoose home with us to stay to-night, and bring her home to-morrow: if you are my friend, you will now show me."

The feelings of the grandfather at once uprose in his bosom, and the child's mother started with horror and alarm at the thought of entrusting her darling prattlet with the rude tenants of the forest. The question was full of interest. On the one hand, the necessity of placing unlimited confidence in the savage, and entrusting the welfare and the life of his grandchild with him; on the other the certain enmity of a man of influence and consequence in his nation, and one who had been the open enemy of his countrymen in their recent struggle. But he made the decision with a sagacity which showed that he properly estimated the character of the person he was dealing with. He believed that by placing implicit confidence in him, he should command the sense of honor which seems peculiar to the uncontaminated Indian. He told him to take the child; and as the mother, scarcely suffering it to be parted from her, relinquished it into the hands of the old man's wife, he soothed her fears with his assurances of confidence in their promises. That night, however, was a long one; and during the whole of the next morning, many and often were the anxious glances cast upon the pathway leading from Oriskany, if possible to discover the Indians and their little charge, upon their return to its home. But no Indians came in sight. It at length became high noon; all a mother's fears were aroused; she could scarcely be restrained from rushing in pursuit of her loved one. But her father represented to her the gross indignity which a suspicion of their intentions would arouse in the breast of the chief; and half frantic though she was, she was restrained.

The afternoon slowly wore away, and still nothing was seen of her child. The sun had nearly reached the western horizon, and the mother's heart had swollen beyond further endurance, when the forms of the Indian chief and his wife, bearing upon her shoulders their little visiter, greeted its mother's vision. The dress which the child had worn from home had been removed, and in its place its Indian friends had substituted a complete suit of Indian garments, so as completely to metamorphose it into a little squaw. The sequel of this adventure was the establishment of a most ardent attachment and regard on the part of the Indian and his friends for the white settlers. The child, now Mrs. Eells of Missouri, the widow of the late Nathaniel Eells of Whitesboro, still remembers some incidents occurring on the night of her stay at the wigwam, and the kindness of her Indian hostess.

Another—which occurred in relation to the siege of Fort Stanwix, and which evinced the fortitude and prowess of General Schuyler, in moments of difficulty.

When Colonel Willett and his companion Lieutenant Stockwell left the fort and got beyond the investing party, which was not done without passing through sleeping groups of savages, who lay with their arms at their side, they crossed the river, and found some horses running wild in the woods. They were soon mounted, and with the aid of their bark bridles, stripped from the young trees, they made considerable progress on their journey. It is well known that they reached Stillwater village, and begged a reinforcement. General Schuyler, who then quartered in the house of Dirck Swart, Esq., now standing at the foot of the hill, and occupied by Mrs. Williams, called a council of his officers, and asked their advice. It is perhaps not generally known that he was opposed by them. As he walked about in the greatest anxiety, urging them to come to his opinion, he overheard some of them saying, "he means to weaken the army." The emotions of the veteran were always violent at the recollection of this charge. At the instant when he heard the remark, he found that he had bitten a pipe, which he had been smoking, into several pieces, without being conscious of what he had done. Indignantly he exclaimed, "Gentlemen, I shall take the responsibility upon myself; where is the brigadier that will take command of the relief? I shall beat up for volunteers to-morrow." The brave, the gallant, the ill-fated Arnold, started up with his characteristic quickness, and offered to take command of the expedition. In the morning the drum beat for volunteers, and two hundred hardy fellows capable of withstanding great fatigue, offered their services, and were accepted. The result of his efforts is well known; a stratagem, as before mentioned, was played off upon the Tories and Indians, which left St. Leger no alternative but a hasty retreat. To General Schuyler's promptness and fearlessness, therefore, due credit should be given.

The retreat of St. Leger, with the success of the American arms at Bennington, restored hope and animation. Tryon county, smiling through her tears, obeyed with alacrity the call to reinforce General Gates in the month of September following. Her militia mounted on horseback, some without saddles, others without bridles, sallied forth. If as uncouth in their appearance, they were equally as zealous, as the knight of La Mancha.

It is not our province to inquire into the policy or propriety of the change of commanders of the northern army. General Schuyler was always a favorite with the inhabitants of New York. Those few survivors, who have come down to us, the relics of his day, still cherish his name in grateful remembrance. Tryon county owed much to his vigilance and attention. He rejoiced with her when she rejoiced, and wept with her when she wept. Alive to her exposed situation, he was always ready to afford relief so far as it could be done consistently.

Another—in relation to the same siege may be interesting to the reader.

A man by the name of Baxter, who resided in the vicinity of the fort, being a disaffected man, had been sent to Albany, to be watched by the committee of safety. Two sons of his remained behind, and were extremely industrious, taking every opportunity to keep their farm in order, notwithstanding its being in the vicinity of the hostile parties. They were so successful, and so little disturbed by the British, that the Americans began to suspect that they were on too good terms with the enemy. Their father's character kept up the suspicion. One day, as it subsequently appeared, one of the sons, who was working with a wheel plough, in cutting his furrows, would every few minutes approach a fence which was between him and the enemy. After several turns, as he was making his last cut across the field, he felt his hands suddenly grasped with violence. Impelled by a natural desire to escape, he jumped forward, and seizing his plough cleaver, he turned on his antagonist, who was an Indian, and felled him to the ground. But a second approached, and with equal dexterity and nerve he dealt a second blow, which levelled the savage. Both were stunned, their heads being too obvious to escape the terrible blow of the plow cleaver. As they lay on the ground, he alternately struck them over the heads with all his might, and then setting his horses clear from the plough, he came to the fort and told them what had happened. His tale was not believed, and when he offered to lead them to the spot, they suspected further treachery. They detained him to abide the event, and sent out a detachment to ascertain how the fact was; and these found two savages lying dead at the place he mentioned. This brave feat procured the release of the father, and indeed rescued the whole family from the imputation of toryism forever.

Another—respecting Abraham D. Quackenboss, as being connected with the battle of Oriskany, may also be interesting.

Abraham D. Quackenboss, resided in the Mohawk country on the south side of the river, at the breaking out of the war. Living as it were among the Indians, he spoke their language as well as he did his own. Among them he had a friend, named Bronkahorse—who, though an Indian, had been his playmate, and they had served in the French war together under Sir William Johnson. When the revolutionary troubles came on, Bronkahorse called upon Quackenboss, and endeavored to persuade him to espouse the cause of the King—assuring him that their *Great Father* could never be conquered. Quackenboss refused, and they parted. The Indian, however, assuring him that they parted as friends, although, since they had fought in one war together he had hoped they might do so in the other. Mr. Quackenboss saw no more of his friend until the battle of Oriskany. During the thickest of the fight he heard his name called in the well known voice of Bronkahorse, from behind a large tree near by. He was himself sheltered by a tree; but in looking out for the warriors he saw his Indian friend. The latter now importuned Quackenboss to surrender, assuring him of kind treatment and protection, but also assuring him unless he did so, he would inevitably be killed. Quackenboss refused, and the Indian thereupon attempted to kill him. For a moment they watched each other endeavoring to obtain the first and best chance of a shot. The Indian at length fired, and his ball struck the tree, but had nearly been fatal. Springing from his covert upon the Indian, Quackenboss fired, and his friend Bronkahorse fell dead on the spot. It was the belief of Mr. Quackenboss that the loss of the enemy during that battle equalled that of Herkimer's command. The latter suffered the most severely in the early part of the engagement—the enemy in the latter part.

About the time of the investment of Fort Stanwix the following incident occurred:

Captain Gregg went with two of his soldiers into the woods a short distance to shoot pigeons; a party of Indians started suddenly from their concealment in the bushes, shot them all down, tomahawked and scalped them and left them for dead. The Captain after some time revived, and perceiving his men were killed, himself robbed of his scalp, and suffering extreme agony from his numerous wounds, made an effort to move, and laying his bleeding head on one of the dead bodies, expected soon to expire. A faithful dog who had accompanied him manifested great agitation, and in the tenderest manner possible licked his wounds, which afforded him great relief from exquisite distress. He then directed the dog, as if a human being, to go in search of some person to come to his relief. The animal with every appearance of anxiety, ran about a mile, where he met with two men a fishing in the river, and endeavored in the most moving manner, by whining and piteous cries to prevail on them to follow into the woods. Struck with the singular conduct of the dog, they were induced to follow him part of the way; but fearing some decoy, or danger, they were about to return, when the dog fixing his eyes on them renewed his entreaties by his cries, and taking hold of their clothes with his teeth, prevailed on them to follow him to the fatal spot. Such was the remarkable fidelity and sagacity of this animal. Captain Gregg was immediately carried to the fort, where his wounds were dressed. He was a most frightful spectacle; the whole of his scalp was removed; in two places on the fore part of his head the tomahawk had penetrated the skull; there was a wound on his back with the same instrument, besides a wound in his side, and another through his arm by a musket ball. This unfortunate man, after suffering extremely for a long time, finally recovered and appeared to be well satisfied in having his scalp restored to him, though uncovered with hair.

About the same time three young girls who were engaged in picking berries were fired upon by the Indians. Two of them were killed and scalped, and the third made her escape, wounded by two balls shot through her shoulder. The foregoing statements need no comment. The men who employed such instruments, and who stimulated them by promises and rewards, have received the just execration of an indignant people.

CHAPTER III

During this interval, Burgoyne exerted himself with extreme diligence in opening a passage from Fort Ann to Fort Edward. But notwithstanding the ardor with which the whole army engaged in the work, their progress was extremely slow; so formidable were the obstacles which nature as well as art had thrown in their way. Besides having to remove the fallen trees with which the Americans had obstructed the roads, they had no less than forty bridges* to construct, and many others to repair. Finally the army encountered so many impediments in measuring this inconsiderable space, that it could not arrive on the banks of the Hudson, near Fort Edward, until the twenty-eighth of July. General Schuyler, deeming his forces insufficient, in the present state of the fort, to oppose so powerful an army, and being apprehensive that Colonel St. Leger, after the reduction of Fort

---

* These bridges, especially across the marshes, were principally constructed of logs laid parallel and contiguous to one another, and covered with evergreen boughs; many of the logs remain entire even to this day.

Schuyler, might descend by the left bank of the Mohawk to the Hudson and thus intercept his retreat, abandoned Fort Edward, and retired down the river to Stillwater where he remained a few days and then proceeded on to Van Shaick's Island* near Waterford, where he encamped with his army, and threw up numerous fortifications on that and Hauver Island. The left wing under General Arnold, and composed of two brigades and Colonel Morgan's rifle corps, was stationed at Loudon's ferry, on the south bank of the Mohawk, five miles above its confluence with the Hudson, to prevent Burgoyne from crossing at that place, should his march be continued thus far towards Albany. That event, however, was not destined to happen.

* As a visit to "Bemis's Heights" has become a subject of increasing interest, and as the question, among numerous others, is frequently asked by people from all parts of the Union, who are not acquainted with the facts, why the American army, while under the command of General Schuyler, encamped on and fortified Van Schaick's Island, with any expectation of opposing Burgoyne in his march to Albany; I will for the information of the public generally, give the following explanation:

At that time, there were no bridges across either the Hudson or Mohawk, nor were there ferries as plenty as they have been

At the same time the Americans evacuated Fort George, having previously burned their vessels upon the lake, and interrupted in various places the road that leads thence to Fort Edward. The route from Ticonderoga to this fortress by Lake George was thus left entirely open by the Americans. The English, upon their arrival on the Hudson river, which had been so long the object of their wishes, and which had been at length obtained at the expense of so many trials and hardships, were

---

since; the only ferry on the Mohawk, between the Hudson river and Schenectady was Loudon's, about five miles above its mouth, where Arnold was posted with the left wing of the American army, for the purpose of preventing a passage at that place. There was another ferry near Halfmoon Point, (Waterford), across the Hudson, but that would only have been leading him out of the way on the opposite side of the river; besides, the conveying so large an army over that stream in a common scow-boat, and at the same time subject to be opposed by the Americans who lay near by, would have rendered such an undertaking impracticable. Those being the facts, his course necessarily lay across the "Sprouts," as they were called, or mouths of the Mohawk, which, except in time of freshets, were fordable, and by four of which that stream enters the Hudson; the second and third forming Van Schaick's Island, across which the road passed, and was the usual route at that time.

seized with a delirium of joy, and persuaded themselves that victory could now no longer escape them. But ere it was long, their brilliant hopes were succeeded by anxiety and embarrassment.

On the near approach of Burgoyne with so powerful, and as yet successful an army, with his horde of unrestrained savages, who were continually in advance and on his flanks, prowling about the country, plundering, murdering, and scalping all who refused loyalty to the British king; the inhabitants on both sides of the river in the wildest consternation and alarm, fled in every direction. The horrors of war, however mitigated by the laws and usages of civilization, are at all times sufficiently terrific; but when to these the fierce cruelties of a cloud of savages are superadded, those only who are familiar with an American border warfare, can form an adequate opinion of its atrocities. In one place a long cavalcade of ox carts occasionally intermixed with wagons, filled with all kinds of furniture hurriedly thrown in, and not often selected by the owners with reference to their use or value, on occasions of such alarm, were stretched for some distance along the road; while in another might be seen a number on horseback, and here and there two mounted at once on a steed panting under the weight of a double load, closely followed by a crowd of pedestrians, and some perhaps weeping mothers, with a child or two screaming in their arms or on their backs, trudging along with fearful and hurried step. These found great difficulty in keeping up with the rapid flight of their mounted friends. Here and there would be seen some humane person assisting the more unfortunate, by relieving them of their burthens, with which they were encumbered; but generally a principle of selfishness prevented much interchange of friendly offices—every one for himself was the common cry.

To those who now sit quietly under their own shady bowers, or by the fireside long endeared by tranquility and happiness, it is left to imagine, with what feelings they hastened to abandon their homes and their all, as it were, and fly for safety, they knew not whither. The men of this generation can never know what were the sorrows of those fathers that saw their children exposed to dangers and death, and what the agonies of those kind mothers, of whom my own respected mother was one, who pressed their offspring to their bosoms in the constant apprehension of seeing them torn from their embraces, to become the victims of savage cruelty. And it is impossible with sufficient force to describe the appalling distress that many families experienced at that moment of peril and alarm.

Burgoyne, always moved with great precaution, was always seeking intelligence, and if ever a general was well served by his scouts, or an invading army assisted by disaffected inhabitants, his was. Rank toryism and infamous venality fought against us on his side; and if we had not been sustained by the Lord of battles, we should have sunk under the many difficulties that beset us. And it is a well known fact, that the ancestors of some respectable families in this vicinity, were actively engaged in their secret exertions in favor of Burgoyne.

Among the numerous acts of savage cruelties committed by the Indians, was the tragical death of Miss Jane McCrea; an event which drew tears from every eye, and might furnish, if not too horrible, an affecting subject for the painter or dramatist; and which contributed soon after in a powerful degree, to excite the mass of the Americans to rise against the British army. The following account of this tragedy, received through the politeness of Mr. William T. Baker, of Sandy Hill, corresponds, in all the essential particulars, with the often repeated accounts given to me by my much respected parents, who were familiarly acquainted with Miss McCrea, and who received their information from those who were eye witnesses to the scene.

The names of David Jones and Jane M'Crea are indelibly impressed upon the page of American liberty, and the tragic fate of the latter forms an interesting and melancholy incident of the memorable wars of the Revolution. It has accordingly furnished a fruitful theme for fancy and "poetic imaginings," as well as for the graver and more authentic details of history. It has occurred to me that, after so much poetry and fable, the public would be gratified with a plain narrative of the truth of the lamentable transaction. This I think the more desirable, inasmuch as the published histories of this tragedy are both defective, and in some essential particulars incorrect. I have therefore obtained from Caleb Baker, Esq., a resident of the village of Sandy Hill, who was born where he now resides, five years before the Revolution, (in April, 1771) a minute and authentic relation of this Indian scene, with many of the attending circumstances. Mr. C. Baker was not an eye witness of "the catastrophe," for he was then a lad of six years of age, and was at the time at Stillwater, to which place his father, Albert Baker, Esq., had removed his family, on the 12th of July, 1777, soon after the evacuation of Ticonderoga by the American army under General St. Clair, and on the 15th of the same month he returned to his house at Sandy Hill, (leaving his family at Stillwater) which stood at the southern extremity of the present village, just two miles north of Fort Edward, and remained there till the 26th July, the day previous to Jane's murder, and fled to Fort Edward with the retreating fragments of scouts and detachments from its feeble garrison. From that place, then in plain view of the scene, he saw Jane shot from her horse by the Indians. On that day no one dared venture from the fort, but at early dawn of the morning of the 28th, Mr. A. Baker, in company with a file of men from the fort, went in search of the body of Jane, and found it naked and mutilated, within about twenty rods of the spot where they had seen her fall the day before, together with the body of an American officer, both stripped and scalped, and rolled down the declivity of the hill, against a large pine tree which had fallen longitudinally along the slope of the ravine, and partially covered with brush. They were borne immediately to the fort which the Americans evacuated that morning, and a small detachment preceded the retreating Americans, with the two bodies, to the right bank of a small creek about three miles below Fort Edward, in time to bury them in a rude and hasty grave before the main body came up. Mr. Baker accompanied the retreating Americans to Stillwater, and then related to his family and friends, among the number of whom were the author's parents, the melancholy fate of poor Jane, and all he had seen and done. This relation has been a thousand times repeated by Mr. Baker, (and perhaps as often by the author's parents) whose memory is like a book, and as faithful and true as the record. Neither Mr. C. Baker nor his father, A. Baker, found the murdered Jane while still "breathing," nor was she buried under the celebrated pine tree yet standing and commonly shown as marking the spot where she was butchered. Nor was she found by her lover, a "reeking corse," and transported in a baggage wagon to Moses-kill, and there buried by the orders of the British "general officers," as stated by a correspondent of the "Mirror." Nor were the Indians surprised by an American scout crossing the river within sixty or eighty rods of them, and in their hurry and trepidation induced to murder her. There was no such scout. Every American not under British protection, that could reach the fort, had already fled to it, and none dared leave it on that day. There were no American troops or militia on the west side of the river, and the fort was on the east bank. There were no Americans, therefore, to cross from the west to the east bank toward the Indians. The Indians had the wilderness and the field alone to themselves.

Miss M'Crea was the daughter of a New-Jersey clergyman, who on the death of her mother married a second wife, and Jane came to reside with her brother, John M'Crea, who had already settled himself some five or six

years before the war, on the western bank of
the Hudson, about six miles below Fort Edward. This whole country was then an unknown wilderness, and Mr. M'Crea, the brother
of Jane, was one of the pioneer settlers.
Five miles farther up the river, and on the
same bank, and within one mile of Fort Edward, was also located the *Widow Jones*, with
a family of six sons, who also emigrated from
New-Jersey some few years before the war.
These sons were Jonathan, John, Dunham,
Daniel, David (our hero) and Solomon. Three
of these were already married and settled in
the adjoining towns. John in Kingsbury,
near three miles north of Sandy Hill, in what
is now called Moss street. I mention this as
marking the spot near which there was considerable skirmishing between the advance of
the British army and Indians and the flying
Americans, where several of the latter were
killed on the 26th of July aforesaid. A very
small part of the country was at this time
thinly settled with emigrants, some from New
Jersey, as before stated, and some from New
England. Feeling their own feeble and defenceless condition, and what they deemed the
irresistible power of Great Britain, with the

exception of the New England emigrants, and Mr. A. Baker, these scattered settlers were tories and loyalists, and on the breaking out of the Revolution some fled to Canada, and many who remained accepted British protection on the approach of Burgoyne's army. Among many others, the Joneses proved to be tories, and fled to Canada immediately after Burgoyne's capture. In the fall of 1776, Jonathan and David raised a company of fifty or sixty men, under the pretext of reinforcing the American garrison at Ticonderoga, but they passed by the American fort and joined the British post at Crown Point, about fifteen miles farther down the lake. In the winter, Jonathan and David repaired to Canada, and obtained commissions in the British service—Jonathan as captain and David as lieutenant in the same company; and they accompanied Burgoyne's invading army as pilots and pioneers against their own country.

Miss Jane M'Crea was at this time about twenty-three years of age, and David Jones somewhat older. It is supposed that they had been acquainted in New-Jersey. At any rate an intimacy had grown up between the *young folks* in the solitude of the wilderness, from which common report had inferred reciprocal love and the usual implied contract. On the twenty-sixth of July, Burgoyne had penetrated with his main army through the wilderness and clay of Kingsbury, and his advance under General Frazer was encamped on a small elevation about a mile north of the house of John Jones before mentioned. The skirmish, as before stated took place this day, and the outposts and scouting parties of the Americans were driven in and sought refuge in Fort Edward, from the tomahawk and scalping knife of the Indians. By this time it would seem that Jane was somewhat apprised of the proximity of her lover. But all this is matter of inference suggested by her movements. On this day Jane came from her brother's residence to the house of Peter Freel ("the old Baldwin house,") who lived close under the walls of the fort, and remained there the succeeding night. The next morning, after breakfast, she repaired to the house of Mrs. M'Niel, (afterwards Mrs. Campbell,) own cousin and intimate acquaintance of General Frazer, and who had recently emigrated from Scotland. This house stood about eighty rods north of the fort, at the point of junction with the main

road, to a foot walk leading in a direct
from the fort to an old breastwork on the
hill—overlooking the fort from the foot of
second hill. There was a marsh separa[ted]
from the river by ground somewhat eleva[ted]
and joining its eastern bank, on which F[ort]
Edward was erected. On the morning of [the]
27th our people in the fort sent out a rec[on]
noitering party of about fifty men, under [the]
command of Lieutenant Palmer, to ascert[ain]
the position and watch the motions of [the]
enemy. They seem to have proceeded on
the plain about a mile north of the fort, wh[en]
on entering a deep ravine near the river, t[hey]
fell into an ambuscade, or met a party of [In]
dians of about two hundred, and immedia[tely]
fled for their lives towards the fort. [The]
Indians pursued and shot down and sca[lped]
eighteen of them. The Americans ru[shed]
out of the plain and precipitated thems[elves]
down the hill and across the marsh, on [the]
foot walk above mentioned, and such a[s es]
caped, returned to the fort. Near the [foot]
of the hill, the Indians shot down the [com]
mander of the American party, and the
private fell upon the causeway adjoining [the]
foot walk aforesaid. Six of the Indians ru[shed]

forward across the said marsh to the house of Mrs. M'Neil, (Campbell) where Jane had already repaired, as before stated. They seized them both and hurried them back, retracing their steps, and rejoined the main body at the foot of the hill. There they placed Jane on a horse, which seems to have been provided for the occasion, and reascended the hill. All their motions were intently watched from the fort, and at this point, the discharge of some rifles were heard, and Jane was seen to fall from her horse. The operation of the tomahawk and scalping knife were quickly performed, and the body soon dragged forward out of sight of the fort. This scene was enacted about mid-day, and the next morning the bodies of Jane and the American officer were recovered and disposed of in the manner I have already related.

The cause of this unprovoked and barbarous Indian butchery, has never been satisfactorily explained, and has always been, and ever will remain the subject of various and discordant conjecture.

About one hundred of the Indians were of the St. Regis tribe, and another hundred of the St. Aux Geest, or some other tribe; and here the two parties quarrelled about the honor or profits, or both, of taking her into camp; one leader shot her from the horse, and the other scalped her. From the necessity of the case, we must take their own account of the matter, if they ever rendered any, or that of Mrs. M'Neil, (Campbell), whose horror and alarm must have incapacited her for just observation. There is no evidence that she ever gave any explanation of the transaction. To her, it seems, they were indeed rough and ungenteel gallants. In their route back to the camp, they pursued the track of the lumber road, leading from Kingsbury to the fort, about a mile east of the village of Sandy Hill. On this road, distant two miles from the fort, there lived William Griffin, a tory, who had a protection from Burgoyne. The Indians stopped at this house, exhibited their scalps and said they "had killed Jenny." Among the rest they displayed her scalp. They had Mrs. Campbell (M'Neil with them, in a state of perfect nudity, with the exception of her *chemise*, and when they departed they took Griffin with them, but offered no other violence. This part of the story is furnished by Sal. Griffin, as she was *then and is still called,* who was then a girl of twelve years of age, living with her father. She still lives in or near the village of Sandy Hill, and is "the female attendant" spoken of by the correspondent of the Mirror. But the young ladies of this then wilderness had no female "attendants," and on this occasion, poor Jane had no female *companion,* but old Mrs. M'Neil, (Campbell) The Indians delivered her in the condition I have described, to her cousin General Frazer, who was much perplexed and embarrased to provide a suitable robe for so corpulent a lady.

The Joneses are said to have deserted Burgoyne before the capture, and David is related to have died in Canada about three years after of a broken heart. It is also said, and probably with much truth, by those who pretend to authentic information, that he rushed into the midst of the battle of the 19th of September on Bemis's Heights, and was there slain.

The following suggestions to this narrative may tend to elucidate the transactions related:

The Indians, supposed by Mr. Baker to be different tribes, were but different sections of the same tribe; occupying the two branches of the St. Lawrence at the confluence of the St.

Regis river. St. Regis is the English pronunciation, and St. Aux Geest the Yankee sound of the French pronunciation of the same name. The efforts to account for the murder of Miss M'Crea, by ferocious savages, furious with the recent onslaught, and whose keen appetites were sharpened by fresh blood, are palpable absurdities; and imply a total forgetfulness of their known rule of warfare, and indiscriminate and unsparing slaughter. The inducements to strip and plunder Mrs. M'Neil, —(Campbell) were sufficient to account for the butchery of Miss M'Crea. The idea of Jones sending an Indian scout for Miss M'Crea is preposterous. It was not only ungallant, but wholly unnecessary for her safety. All who were so disposed, received protection from Burgoyne, and remained unmolested by the British or Indians. The Whig Americans had enough to do to take care of themselves, and had neither license nor inclination to punish the *loyalty* of the majority. Jones knew that Fort Edward would be evacuated on the approach of the British army, and Jane would have been found safe at Mrs. M'Neil's or at her brother's house. It is probable, therefore, that Jane intended to avail herself of the protection of Mrs. M'Neil, whose loyalty and consanguinity were ample guaranties of her safety, and came to the house for the purpose; and both she and the old lady would have awaited there, the approach of General Frazer, had it not been for the unfortunate movement between the American scouts and the marauding Indian party on the morning of her death. The horse was more probably stolen than provided for Jane's comfort or convenience; and had they been sent to the house of Mrs. M'Neil, General Frazer would have been made acquainted with the design, and would have provided for her as well as for Jane. The place of the rencontre too, forbids the presumption, that this Indian party was sent to escort these two ladies to the British camp. They were lurking in ambuscade, in a deep ravine, some distance from the highway, between that and the river where they had been seen early that morning, by a Tory who lived near the spot, for the very purpose, no doubt, of intercepting any American scouts or vedets. They pressed forward to the house of Mrs. M'Niel, because they were near it; and it was out of reach of the guns of the garrison, more probably for plunder or the scalps of the flying

Americans, (some of whom they might have supposed to have taken refuge in the house) than for the ladies whom they carried off and treated as prisoners.

Miss M'Crea's name is inscribed on the west side of the pine tree before mentioned, with the date 1777, and no traveller passes this spot without spending a plaintive moment in contemplating the untimely and tragical fate of youth and loveliness, and dropping a silent tear in token of the inward workings of a sensitive mind.

At the time of her death she was about twenty-three years of age, of midling stature, finely formed, dark hair, and uncommonly beautiful. About the same time, Mr. John Allen, of the town of Argyle, his wife, three children, and three negroes (the property of his father-in-law) were all murdered by the Indians. The negroes were sent for the purpose of assisting Mr. Allen in the harvest field, and it is supposed they were all murdered while at dinner. Allen and his father-in-law, Mr. Gilmer, were both Tories; this created a great alarm among the Tories of Argyle, and they flocked in great numbers to Sandy-Hill to solicit from Burgoyne protection against the marauding savages. Upon which General Frazer made the following remark, "It is a conquered country, and we must wink at such things." The Tories remonstrated, and Burgoyne having issued orders that those who held protections from him must not be molested, a number of the Indians left him and returned to Canada.

General Gates in a letter addressed to General Burgoyne, thus spoke of the cases above cited:—Miss M'Crea, a young lady, lovely to the sight, of virtuous character and amiable disposition, engaged to an officer of your army, was, with other women and children, taken out of a house at Fort Edward, carried into the woods, and there scalped and mangled in the most shocking manner. Two parents, with their six children, were treated with the same inhumanity, while quietly resting in their own happy and peaceful dwelling. The miserable fate of Miss M'Crea was particularly aggravated, by being dressed to receive her promised husband; but met her murderers, employed by you. Upwards of one hundred men, women and children have perished by the hand of the ruffians, to whom, it is asserted, you have paid the price of blood.

The British commander, in his reply to General Gates, labored at some length, to make the best of his case, and, among other things, had the effrontery to say, that excepting the foregoing instance, his intelligence respecting the cruelty of the Indians was false.

The effect of the incidents we have been detailing, and other recitals of savage cruelties, not all, as General Burgoyne represented, without foundation, was extensive and powerful. The cry of vengence was universal; and a spirit was aroused which proved of speedy and great advantage to the American arms.

Often, when a boy, have I sat long and silent, in the family group, by the side of my much respected, now sainted mother, listening to her tales of alarm, suffering and distress, that pervaded this part of the country, in those troublous times; and the dangers to which she herself had frequently been exposed. And often while reciting the tragic fate of her friend and acquaintance, Miss Jane M'Crea, and other equally savage cruelties, have I seen the "big tear" roll from her glistening eye and trickle down her cheek, glowing with the emotions of her heart. And even to this day, when I reflect on those scenes of savage cruelty, and with what emotion they were then recited, a sympathetic tear will insensibly steal from my eye, and I am involuntarily led to exclaim O! my mother! my much loved mother! could I have been present to have witnessed those scenes of danger and alarm to which thou hast been exposed, and from which thou barely escaped with thy life, with one arm would I have encircled that brow, around which the Indian's tomahawk thrice was brandished, preparatory to the fatal stroke; and with the other would I have *dashed* to the earth, that ferocious savage, whose scalping-knife, reeking with the blood of thy friends, was already drawn to execute on thee its threatened deed! But a mightier arm was interposed for thy protection —He in whom thou thou trusted was there—for at the critical moment, when there seemed no possible escape, a file of men approached, as if specially and providentially directed—the sharp crack of rifles was heard in the distance —the fatal balls were sped—two cruel savages fell dead at thy feet, and thou alone, the joy of thy friends, wast saved, to relate the sad story of thy three murdered companions!

It may be supposed from my relation of so many of the numerous scenes, and some of

>'Tis faith thus wrought, whose fearful mysteries
>Yield e'en weak woman strength for deeds like these.

them heart-rending, through which my own friends have passed, that *they* were the only persons who suffered in those trying times. My intention is not to be so understood, nor do I suppose that the many trials through which they passed, were greater than those of many others; yet the relation of them, by being often repeated, have become more familiar, and consequently better enables me to give a correct account of them.

The subsequent tragic scene, though I do not now recollect all the particulars, I will recount in substance, as follows:—

My step-grandfather, had been very active among the Indians and Tories, and understood their manner of warfare so well, that he was often selected to head volunteer parties, who went in pursuit of them, in their marauding expeditions, and was generally very successful; for which they owed him a grudge, and tried many ways to decoy and take him; but he had always eluded them.

It happened on a time when it was supposed there were no Indians in the vicinity, and the inhabitants all felt secure, that my father was gone from home on business with the committee of safety, leaving my grandfather, grandmother, and mother, at home alone—they all occupying the same house at the time. Soon after dark, a little dog which they had, and which was then in the house, for some moments seemed to express considerable uneasiness, and at last ran to the door, and with a kind of howl, or unusual expression, immediately turned and looked up, with much seeming concern, to my grandfather, whose keen perception in a moment led him to exclaim, "Indians!" He immediately caught his rifle, which lay horizontally on hooks attached to a beam overhead, and opening the door stepped out. But he had no sooner passed the threshhold, than the sharp crack of three rifles were heard in rapid succession, and he staggered back, exclaiming, "Run for your lives!" and fell into the room. My mother and grandmother, already horror-stricken, gave a sudden scream and immediately sprang out of an opposite window, and ran to a neighboring house, about eighty rods distant, to give the alarm. It so happened that two distant neighbors, who had been out that day on a hunting excursion, called at the same house some ten or fifteen minutes before, and hearing the firing, were, in company with the occupant, listening to ascertain its direction, if repeated. At the same time a horse was heard at a distance rapidly approaching, which soon proved to be my father's, on which, having heard the firing, and suspecting mischief, he was riding at the top of his speed, and arrived at the moment the alarm was given. Springing from his horse, and being furnished with a rifle, the four men immediately hurried on, regardless of any danger they might be rushing into. On approaching the house, it being then quite dark, they caught the glimpse of persons running in the direction of a piece of woods near by; upon whom they, in their hurry, fired at random.

Having pursued on to the skirt of the wood, and seeing no more of the enemy, they returned to the house, where a mournful spectacle presented itself. There lay the mangled and lifeless corpse of my grandfather, drenched in his own blood, and tomahawked and scalped; and on examination it was found that three balls had passed through his body. In searching, the next morning, at the place where the

Indians, for such were they supposed to be, were fired upon, they found blood in several places leading into the woods, evincing that some *one* of them, at least, had been wounded. It was supposed that the hostile party consisted of four Tories, and five Indians, as that number was seen next day, near Fort Edward, travelling north with a hurried step; one of which limped considerably and lagged behind.

A short time previous to the foregoing tragedy, my grandfather, at the head of fifty men, had a desperate encounter with about eighty Indians and Tories at Sabbathday Point,* in which the enemy were defeated, with the loss of forty killed and wounded. It was supposed that, in consequence of so signal a defeat, which was effected by means of an ambuscade, the Indians and Tories were determined,

---

* Sabbathday Point is a low neck of land stretching into Lake George from the western shore, three miles from the little village of Hague. On Sabbathday Point, Lord Amherst with his army stopped for refreshment upon the morning of the Sabbath, and gave this beautiful spot the name by which it is now known. It is a charming spot, and susceptible of great embellishment. In the summer of 1756, a small body of Provincials who had retreated to this point, defeated a superior force of French and Indians, who had attacked them in gun-boats.

at all hazards, to destroy the man, who in this, as in many other instances, had been so great a scourge to them, and which they finally accomplished, in the manner already related.

At the time the American army under General Schuyler was retreating down the Hudson from Fort Edward, small parties of Tories and Indians kept pace with them along the opposite bank, and when an opportunity presented, where the road was on or near the margin of that stream, along which the army passed, they would secrete themselves near the bank and fire across at the officers and men; and in this manner they pursued them as far down as Stillwater, wounding many on the way. When the army was thus passing near E. Vandenburgh's, and opposite a shoal place in the river, an Indian waded out some distance and fired, hitting a soldier and badly wounding him in the hand. Another soldier, by the name of Dirk Van Vechten, who was marching in the same platoon, was so vexed at it that he was determined to avenge the injury. Accordingly he kept a sharp look out, and watching his opportunity, as soon as he saw an Indian approach the river, he crept along on the ground, and laid himself down on the margin of the bank, behind some open bushes; and as an Indian arrived at a spot in the river from which he raised his piece to fire, Van Vechten let drive at him, when the Indian bounded, with a horrid screech, three feet out of water and fell, and he saw no more of him. After that, the Indians were very careful how and where they showed themselves.

CHAPTER IV

The progress of Burgoyne thoroughly alarmed the American states also; it being well known that the American forces under General Schuyler were not sufficient to prevent the capture of Albany, whenever it was reached by the enemy. Instead of thinking of submission, the Americans met this alarming crisis with firmness and resolution, and great exertions were made to reinforce the army. General Lincoln, of Massachusetts, was directed to raise and take command of the New England militia. Colonel Morgan, with his riflemen, was detached to the northern army, and Congress elected General Gates as Commander.

The appointment of General Gates, though he did not assume the command till after the battle of Bennington, created considerable excitement at that time in the public mind, and much dissatisfaction was expressed on account of that measure; and with my limited means of knowledge, I have never been able to learn what good reason induced the removal of Gen. Schuyler. Few men in our country at that time ranked higher, in all the essential qualities of the patriot, the gentleman, the soldier, and scholar. The nobility of soul he possessed, distinguished him from ordinary men, and pointed him out as one deserving of public confidence.

While the American army was thus assuming a more respectable appearance, General Burgoyne was making very slow advances towards Albany. From the 28th of July to the 15th of August, the British army was continually employed in bringing forward batteaux, provisions, and ammunition, from Fort George, to the first navigable part of the Hudson river, a distance of not more than fifteen miles.

The labor was excessive, the Europeans were but little acquainted with the methods of performing it to advantage, and the effect was in no degree equivalent to the expense and time. With all the efforts that Burgoyne could make, encumbered with his immense train of artillery and baggage, his labors were inadequate to the purpose of supplying his army with provisions for its daily consumption, and the establishment of the necessary magazines. And after his utmost exertions for fifteen days, there was not above four days' provisions in store, nor above ten batteaux in the Hudson river.

In such circumstances, the British general found that it would be impossible to procure sufficient supplies of provisions by the way of Lake George, and determined to replenish his own magazines at the expense of those of the Americans. Having received information that a large quantity of stores were laid up at Bennington, and were guarded only by the militia, he formed the design of surprising that place; and was made to believe that as soon as a detachment of the royal army should appear in that quarter, it would receive effectual assistance from a large body of loyalists, who only waited for the appearance of a support, and would in that event, come forward and aid in the royal cause. Full of these expectations, he detached Colonel Baum, a German officer, with a select body of troops, to surprise the place. This force consisted of about five hundred regular troops, some Canadians, and more than one hundred Indians, with two light pieces of artillery. To facilitate their operations, and to be ready to take advantage of the success of the detachment, the royal army moved down along the east bank of the Hudson river, and encamped nearly opposite Saratoga (Schuylerville); having at the same time thrown a bridge of rafts across the river, by which the advanced corps passed to that place. With a view to support Baum, if it should be found necessary, Lieutenant Colonel Breyman's corps, consisting of the Brunswick grenadiers, light infantry and chasseurs, were posted about five miles up the Battenkill.

General Stark having received information that a party of Indians were at Cambridge, sent Lieutenant-Colonel Gregg, on the thirteenth of August, with a party of two hundred men to stop their progress. Towards night he was informed by express that a large body of regulars was in the rear of the Indians, and advancing towards Bennington. On this intelligence, Stark drew together his brigade, and militia that were at hand, and sent to Manchester for Col. Warner to bring on his regiment; he sent expresses at the same time to the neighboring militia, to join him with the utmost speed. On the morning of the fourteenth, he marched with his troops, and at a distance of seven miles he met Gregg on the retreat, and the enemy within a mile of him. General Stark drew up his troops in order of battle; but the enemy coming in sight, halted upon a very advantageous piece of ground. Colonel Baum perceiving the Americans were too strong to be attacked with his present forces, sent an express to Burgoyne with an account of his situation, and to have Breyman march immediately to his support. In the meantime small parties of the Americans kept up a skirmish with the enemy, killed and wounded thirty of them, with two of their Indian chiefs, without any loss to themselves. The ground the Americans had taken was unfavorable for a general action, and Stark retreated about a mile and encamped. A council of war was held, and it was agreed to send two detachments upon the enemy's rear, while the rest of the troops should make an attack upon their front. The next day the weather was rainy, and though it prevented a general action, there were frequent skirmishings in small parties, which proved favorable and encouraging to the Americans.

On the sixteenth of August, in the morning, General Stark was joined by Colonel Symonds and a body of militia from Berkshire, and proceeded to attack the enemy, agreeably to the plan which had been concerted. Colonel Baum, in the meantime, had entrenched on an advantageous piece of ground near St. Koick's mills, on a branch of the Hoosick river; and rendered his post as strong as his circumstances and situation would admit. Colonel Nichols was detached with two hundred men to the rear of his left, Colonel Herrick with three hundred to the rear of his right: both were to join and then make the attack. Colonels Hubbard and Stickney, with two hundred more, were ordered to the right, and one hundred were advanced to the front to draw the attention of the enemy that way. About three o'clock in the afternoon the troops had taken their several positions, and were ready to commence the action. While Nichols and

Herrick were bringing their troops together, the Indians were alarmed at the prospect, and pushed off between the two corps; but received a fire as they were passing, by which three of them were killed and two wounded. Nichols then began the attack, and was followed by all the other divisions; those in the front immediately advanced, and in a few moments the action became general. It lasted about two hours, and was like one continued peal of thunder. Colonel Baum made a brave defence: and the German dragoons after they had expended their ammunition, led by their Colonel, charged with their swords, but they were soon overpowered. Their works were carried on all sides, their two pieces of cannon were taken, Colonel Baum himself was mortally wounded and taken prisoner, and all his men, except a few who had escaped into the woods, were either killed or taken prisoners. The work having been completed by taking the whole party, the militia began to disperse in search of plunder. But in a very short time General Stark received information that a large reinforcement was on their march, and within two miles of him. Fortunately at that moment Colonel Warner came up with his regiment from Manchester. This brave and experienced officer commanded a regiment of Continental troops, which had been raised in Vermont. Mortified that he had not been in the former engagement, he instantly led on his men against Colonel Breyman, and began the second engagement. General Stark collected the militia as soon as possible, and pushed on to his assistance. The action soon became general, and continued with obstinacy on both sides till sunset, when the Germans were forced to give way, and were pursued till dark. They left their two field pieces behind and a considerable number were made prisoners. They retreated in the best manner they could, improving the advantages of the night, to which alone was their escape ascribed.

The following facts may possibly elucidate the circumstances of the foregoing battles.

On the approach of Col. Baum, he had forces enough, had he continued his march, to have taken all the stores that had for some time been accumulating at Bennington, as there were but few militia there at the time; but a Yankee trick, (and what are the Yankees *not* up to?) was played off upon him, as follows. Three men, "true to the core," in whom General Stark placed the most implicit confidence, offered themselves as volunteers, to go to Colonel Baum, who was on his approach, and represent themselves as loyalists, and ask to be taken under his protection, and even offered to take up arms with him, and fight against the Americans; and at the same time represented the Americans to be in strong force at that place, and that if he attempted to proceed, his troops would all be cut to pieces. Upon this information, and placing great confidence in the "honest looks" of these men, Colonel Baum made a halt near the west line of Bennington, in the town of Hoosick, and sent to Burgoyne for reinforcements. General Stark, taking advantage of the delay, collected together from the surrounding country a considerable number of militia, and having sent an express to Manchester for Colonel Warner to come on with the troops under his command, went out to meet Colonel Baum about five miles from Bennington; and having approached to within about a mile and a half of the Hessian camp, he made a halt at Matthews's, where he remained with his troops through the night.

In the meantime the Hessians fortified themselves on quite an elevated hill on the north side of the river, and directly east of the Barnet house. This hill is of quite steep ascent from the river to the top, but of a more gentle slope in every other direction. On the top, in a sort of timber fort, they placed one of their field pieces, and the other on a level patch of ground at the foot of the hill, and near the margin of the river, for the purpose of covering the Tories, who were posted on a small rise of ground, on the opposite side of the river, and who hastily fortified themselves by placing two tier of rails horizontally, and filling the space with flax that grew in the same field. Near the margin of the river, where the road crossed the bridge, and between the battery at the foot of the hill and the Tories' breast work, stood a log cabin well stowed with women attached to the Hessian army, one of which, on the approach of the Americans, in attempting to flee across the bridge to the Hessian hill, was killed by a musket ball.

Along the road on the margin of the river, and leading from Bennington to Hoosick, General Stark ordered a part of his troops to advance; and in order to make as much show as possible, he directed a number who had no arms to fall in with them, to draw the attention of the Hessians that way; while two regiments were directed by a circuitous route through the woods, to gain the enemy's rear; the plan was well concerted and promptly executed. The Hessians, being now attacked in front and rear, fought for sometime with desperation, till at length, being too hotly pressed, they threw down their arms and fled; but were immediately pursued by the Americans, and nearly all killed or taken prisoners. The day was hot and sultry, and the men, after a long and arduous conflict, were almost exhausted. But, notwithstanding, on the approach of Colonel Breyman with reinforcements, they again rallied as soon as circumstances would permit, and Colonel Warner having arrived with his regiment, prepared for renewed action, and crowned the day with victory complete.

In these actions the Americans took four brass field pieces,* twelve brass drums, two

---

* These beautiful brass pieces of artillery were destined to undergo several of the vicissitudes of war. They are French cast, and were brought from Quebec, with the army of Burgoyne. They were afterwards inscribed, "Taken at Bennington, August 16th, 1777," hundred and fifty dragoon swords, four ammunition wagons, and about seven hundred prisoners, with their arms and accoutrements; two hundred and seven men were found dead upon the field; the number of wounded was not known. The loss of the Americans was but small—thirty were slain, and about forty were wounded.

The consequences of this battle were of great importance. It animated the hearts of the people, more than fulfilling, in this respect, the happy prediction of Washington. But its immediate effects were of the first moment.

and constituted a part of the artillery of General Hull's army, and fell into the enemy's hands at Detroit. When the British officer of the day ordered the evening salutes to be fired from the American cannon, who at the same time reading the inscription, "Taken at Bennington, August 16th, 1777," observed that he would cause to be added as an additional line to the verse, "Retaken at Detroit, August 16th, 1812." The guns were carried by the British down to Fort George, at the mouth of the Niagara river, where they again fell into the hands of the American army, which captured that fortress. General Dearborn had them transported to Sackets-Harbor, and with them was fired the salutes in honor of Harrison's victory over Proctor at the river Thames, in Upper Canada. The guns are now at the city of Washington, where it is hoped they may remain in peace.

It not only cost the army of Burgoyne more than one thousand of his best troops, but it wholly deranged the plan of his campaign, and materially contributed to the loss of his army. By advancing beyond Ticonderoga, his communication with the country in his rear was interrupted. He relied on these lateral excursions to keep the population in alarm, and prevent their flocking to General Schuyler, who at this time had the command of the northern army. He also depended on procuring his supplies by such inroads into the country. The catastrophe of Baum's expedition, by which he hoped to furnish himself with an ample store of provisions collected at Bennington, disappointed that expectation, and compelled him to halt until he could procure them in detail from other quarters, and thus retarded his advance toward Albany for a month; during all which time, the militia poured to the standard of General Schuyler, and placed the Americans in a condition to compel the surrender of the whole British army. In the memoir of Baron Reidesel's expedition, written by the baroness, his lady, it is stated that this judicious officer strongly remonstrated against despatching Col. Baum, and the event of the expedition is declared "to have paralyzed at once the operations of the British army."

After having rendered important services in the arduous campaigns of the French war under Generals Howe, Abercrombie, and Amherst, after sustaining his part gallantly in the fields of Bunker Hill and Trenton, and contributing much to the result of those important actions, General Stark had the mortification to find himself overlooked in the line of promotion, and men who were his inferiors in rank, who had scarcely seen the fire of an enemy, or the smoke of his camp, promoted over him. He remonstrated to Congress, but all to no purpose; and rather than submit to the injustice of the measure, he resigned his commission in the preceding spring, and retired from the army.

When Burgoyne advanced from the north with so powerful a force, and all the energies of the country became necessary to repel his attacks, the authorities of his native state directed their attention to General Stark, relying upon his military reputation and popularity to call out the militia of New Hampshire and

Vermont. At their request, laying aside the recollection of his wrongs, he called upon his friends, the yeomanry of his country, and they obeyed his voice. The victory of Bennington discovered to his astonished countrymen the rare spectacle of undisciplined militia fighting for their firesides and homes, and triumphing over British veterans.

Mr. Jefferson, speaking of himself, General Stark, and Mr. Adams, then the eldest patriarchs of the revolution, in regard to the objects which were most agreeable to the recollections of each of them, makes use of this observation: "Stark talked of his *Bennington,* and exulted in his glory." Exultation in the usual sense of the term, did not belong to him. To all the committees from different states who congratulated him upon his success, his answer was, "that any other man would have done as well under similar circumstances." And well might the hero exult in his fame. He had struck an immortal blow in the cause of Liberty, which turned the tide of conquest against her enemies, and gave hope and confidence to his despairing friends in the common cause. It was not the loud shout of successful ambition, but the honest expression of true patriotism, which characterised his triumph. The liberty of his country was the prize for which he contended—to free the land of his birth from foreign dependence, and not merely the gathering of military laurels, was the object of this soldier citizen; when that was obtained, he retired to domestic life, and never more solicited or received a public employment. It must have been extremely gratifying to his feelings, to observe the effect of his successes upon Congress, late so hostile to his promotion, in drawing from them commissions and votes of thanks.

It is, however, worthy of remark, that while Congress liberally bestowed upon distinguished actors in the great revolutionary drama, swords and medals in approbation of their services, the total defeat of a veteran army, the capture and destruction of a thousand men, and a death blow given to the hopes of the invader, was complimented by the Old Congress, with only a generous vote of thanks bestowed upon the hero of Bennington.

In person General Stark was about the middle size, extremely well proportioned, and in his youth was remarkable for vigor, activity, and the capability of sustaining fatigue; as was proved during the French war, in which a single bearskin and a roll of snow was frequently the war-couch of our gallant veterans. He was a man of kindness and hospitality, which through life he extended to all his broken down companions in arms, and all others who sought his assistance. One remarkable fact in the life of General Stark, is, that although often engaged in close and desperate combat with the French and Indians, and afterwards with the British and Tories, in the Revolution, he was never struck by a shot, or wounded in any manner by the enemy.

His character in his private, was as unexceptionable as in his public life. His manners were frank and open; though tinged with an eccentricity peculiar to himself, and useful to society. He sustained through life, the reputation of a man of honor, and integrity, friendly to the industrous and enterprising—severe to the idle and unworthy—society may venerate the memory of an honest citizen, and the nation of a hero, whose eulogy is written in the remembrance of his countrymen.

Congratulatory letter from General Schuyler to General Stark, written three days after the battle of Bennington.

> VAN SCHAICK'S, Aug. 19th, 1777.
>
> Dear Sir—I do myself the pleasure to congratulate you on the signal victory which you have gained; please accept my best thanks. The consequence of the severe stroke the enemy have received, cannot fail of producing the most salutary results. I have despatched one of my aids-de-camp to announce your victory to Congress and the Commander-in-chief.
>
> Governor Clinton is coming up with a body of militia, and I trust that after what the enemy have received from you, their progress will be retarded, and we shall yet see them driven from this part of the country. General Gates is at Albany, and will this day reassume the command.
>
> I am, dear General,
> Your most obedient,
> PH. SCHUYLER.

Several anecdotes in connection with the battle of Bennington have been recorded, of which the following is one.

Among the reinforcements from Berkshire county came a clergyman, the Rev. Mr. Allen, of Pittsfield, with a portion of his flock, resolved to make bare the arm of flesh against the enemies of the country. Before daylight on the morning of the 16th, he addressed the commander as follows: "We the people of Berkshire have been frequently called upon to fight, but have never been led against the enemy. We have now resolved, if you will not let us fight, never to turn out again." General Stark asked him if he wished to march then, when it was dark and rainy. "No," was the answer. "Then," continued Stark, "if the Lord should once more give us sunshine, and I do not give you fighting enough, I will never ask you to come again." The weather cleared up in the course of the day, and the men of Berkshire followed their spiritual guide into action.

Another—On General Stark's approach to the Hessian camp, and pointing out the enemy to his soldiers, he declared to them that "he wonld gain the victory over them in the approaching battle, or Molly Stark should be a widow that night."

Some two or three days previous to the time that Colonel Baum was detached to Bennington, a party of Indians and Tories were sent on for the purpose of scouring the country between that place and Fort Edward. On their way they captured and took with them Mrs. Hannah Coon, (now Mrs. Grandy) wife of Mr. Elisha Coon, a captain in the American militia, and who was then absent on duty. Mrs. Coon was then in a very delicate situation, and such as required momentary attention; but notwithstanding, she was compelled, as incapacitated as she was, to travel on foot with these ferocious savages and more brutal Tories. The second day after her capture her *accouchment* took place, where they halted for the night. In the morning after her confinement, she, with two other women who had also been captured, was again compelled to walk and carry her child, to the place where the troops under Colonel Baum encamped, previous to the action with the Americans under General Stark. Before the battle, she says, the troops were in high spirits, and boasted much of their ability to subdue the "rebel Yankees" as they called the Americans, and vainly endeavored to persuade a number, whom they had taken prisoners on the way, to join in the cause of the British king. But during the action, and while the soldiers were repeatedly bringing the wounded into camp, she would laugh at, and ridicule them. Soon after the action commenced, she saw the Indians, she says, flying in all directions, and skulking behind trees, rocks, and other places of concealment. On the retreat of the Indians, after the defeat of Colonel Baum, she was taken with them, and soon met the reinforcements under Colonel Breyman; when she returned to camp and remained during the second battle, and was again compelled to travel on foot with them on their retreat to the place where they encamped during the night. Here, owing to her recent confinement and constant fatigue, she was taken sick, and whether it was on that account, or on account of the hurry and bustle the troops were in at the time, being in momentary expectation of pursuit by the Americans, she does not know, but she was left without a guard, and managed to conceal herself and child until they had departed, when she made her escape.

During those days of extreme suffering, distress, and alarm that she experienced, while in her delicate state of health, she was often threatened with instant death, if she refused to proceed or complained of inability; and once in particular, an Indian chief approached her with much ferocity, at a time when she was tantalizing them on their defeat, and actually clenched up her child, which was lying on her lap, and drew his scalping knife around its head, and brandished his tomahawk over her, in token of what he would do if she did not desist; and she thinks would have carried his threats into execution, had it not been for the interference of a humane officer. After her escape, and having undergone all the horrors of a cruel death, she with much difficulty returned home, where she remained alone (excepting her infant child), and in the midst of the wilderness, about three weeks, with nothing to subsist upon but a little salt pork, which had been concealed, and some old or seed cucumbers, that were left undisturbed in the garden, all their other provisions and even her cooking and other furniture having been taken away by the Indians and Tories. The cucumbers she scraped the seeds from and peeled, then roasted them in the embers, and though she was fearful they might kill her, yet, she says, she thought she might as well die by eating them as to starve to death—as the salt pork she could not eat alone.

At the expiration of three weeks she was again taken by the Indians and Tories, who, she thinks, vented their malice particularly upon her, on account of her husband having taken sides with the Americans, as they would often speak of it. At this time she was compelled to cross the river with them, in advance of the British army, and was taken as far as Stillwater, but managed to make her escape during the action of the 19th of September, having suffered much during that time.

But little do the junior matrons of these times of luxury and ease, know or feel of the sufferings and deprivations of those who inhabited this part of the country in those days of peril and alarm; and there are but few, who sufficiently realize the price at which the dear bought liberties of our now happy country were purchased.

Mrs. Coon, (Grandy) now lives on the same farm that her husband owned and occupied when she was taken prisoner—about two miles from Union Village, in Washington county, New York. She is, at the time of writing this narrative, ninety-three years of age, quite active, and her step uncommonly firm for a person of her advanced age; and she bids fair to live yet a number of years. On the recital of her sufferings, a glow of resentment suffused her matronly cheek, and the fire of indignation would sparkle in her keen black eye; but in a moment she sprang upon her feet, with the seeming activity of youth, and broke out in raptures of joy, as though no sacrifice for her country had been too great, and exclaimed with much energy of feeling: "But they got well paid for it! the first army," as she called it, "were most all taken prisoners, and the second got defeated and had to run for their lives;" and "Oh," she says, "how I rejoiced to see it, though I knew my own sufferings would be increased." And who is there so lost to his country's weal as not to exclaim with the patriot poet?

"Amor (patriæ) vincit omnia, et nos cedamus amori."

The following incident took place while Colonel Warner had the command of the garrison at Fort Edward:

While the Americans held undisputed possession of the posts at the north, it was a very common thing for the different commanders to exchange visits. Colonel Warner occasionally visited the commander at Fort George. On

one of these occasions, he was returning with
two officers all of them mounted on horseback.
As they were passing the Bloody Pond, where
some hostile Indians had hid themselves behind
an old tree, they received a volley of musketry
from their concealed enemies. The two officers fell lifeless to the ground, and Colonel
Warner was wounded, as was also the horse
he rode. He put spurs to the bleeding animal
and endeavored to escape. One of the officer's horses accompanied him, and the Indians
pursued. As he rode on, his own occasionally
seemed ready to fall under him, and at other
times would revive and appear to renew his
strength. The other horse kept up with them,
alternately increasing and relaxing his speed,
to keep pace with his wounded companion. The
colonel in vain tried to sieze the bridle which
hung over his neck, an expedient which promised to save him if his own steed should fail.
In this manner, and with all the horrid antici-
pation of a cruel death before him, he managed to outstrip his pursuers until he reached
Glen's Falls. There, as the uninjured horse
came along side, he made another attempt to
seize his bridle, and succeeded. He instantly
dismounted, unslung his own saddle, threw

it over the fence, mounted the other horse and rode off at full speed. He saw no more of his pursuers from this moment, but reached Fort Edward in safety. Not however, without being really overcome by his exertion, fatigue, and loss of blood. What was also singular, was the arrival of his wounded horse, which lived to do good service in the field.

CHAPTER V

Soon after the foregoing battles, General Lincoln, with a strong corps of militia from New Hampshire and Connecticut, conceived the hope of recovering for the States the fortresses of Ticonderoga and Mount Independence, and consequently the command of Lake George. He knew that these places were guarded only by feeble garrisons. He advanced from Manchester to Paulet. He parted his corps into three divisions: the first, commanded by Colonel Brown, was to proceed to the northern extremity of Lake George, and thence to fall by surprise upon Ticonderoga; the second, led by Colonel Johnston, was destined to scour the country about Fort Independence, in order to make a diversion, and even an attack, if occasion should favor it; the third, under the orders of Colonel Woodbury, had it in view to reduce Skeensborough, Fort Ann, and even Fort Edward. Colonel Brown, with equal secresy and celerity, surprised all the posts upon Lake George, and the inlet of Ticonderoga, Mount Hope, Mount Defiance, and the old French lines. He took possession of two hundred batteaux, an armed brig, and several gun boats; he also made a considerable number of prisoners. Colonel Johnston arrived at the same time under the walls of Fort Independence. The two fortresses were summoned to capitulate. But brigadier General Powel, who held the chief command, replied that he was resolved to defend himself. The Americans continued their cannonade for the space of four days; but their artillery being of small calibre, and the English opposing a spirited resistance, they were constrained to abandon the enterprise and to recover their former position.

About the twentieth of August, General Gates, having succeeded to the command of the northern army, soon after left the encampment at Van Schaick's Island, and moved back with it again to Stillwater (Village,) fully determined to face the foe, and if necessary pursue him into his own confines. This was at first supposed to be an eligible position for throwing up a line of entrenchments, and a large party, under an engineer, were accordingly set to work for that purpose. But at the suggestion of the author's father and some others, who were actively engaged at that time, and who were well acquainted with the country, and upon a narrow inspection of the grounds, General Gates determined to change his position and occupy Bemis's Heights, which were immediately taken posession of and fortified. Burgoyne at this time lay nearly opposite to Saratoga, occupying old Fort Miller and the banks of Battenkill near its mouth; but what were his further intentions General Gates had no means of judging. In this situation the deputy Adjutant-General Wilkinson, volunteered to head a select reconnoitering party, and obtain if possible the desired information. He left the camp with one hundred and seventy men, under cover of a dark night (12th Sept.) and arrived by daylight at Do-ve-gat (Cove-Ville) about three miles below Saratoga

(Schuylerville.) Here he posted a greater part of his men in a wood near the road, and proceeded himself to the heights of Fish Creek; from which position he discovered a column of the enemy drawn up under arms on the opposite bank of the creek, within three hundred yards of him, and another column under march descending the heights below Battenkill. Being satisfied, from these circumstances, that General Burgoyne was advancing, Colonel Wilkinson returned to camp with his party, bringing with him three prisoners who confirmed the intelligence.

The following is a description of the ground, [see map] and its vicinity, selected by General Gates, for the encampment of the American army. On the right bank of the Hudson, about three miles above the village of Stillwater, and about twenty-five north of Albany, are extensive alluvial flats, about half a mile in width at the centre, and tapering towards their extremities, until they form a narrow defile of only about thirty rods in width, between the river and the river hills. In the rear of those flats, and even down to their margin, with the exception of here and there a small clearing, and those in the rough, was at that time a dense forest, and in many places for some distance back, the land was much cut up with deep ravines. The only road much traveled at that time, ran along the margin of the river, and through the defile at the southern extremity of those flats, where a man by the name of *Bemis* kept a public house, the only one of any note, I have been informed, between Albany and Fort Edward; and from whom the high land, back, derived the appellation of Bemis's Heights. From these circumstances, an army approaching from the north, and especially with a heavy train of artillery and baggage, was under the necessity of passing along this road, and through this narrow defile. Here and on the Heights, Gates having determined to establish and fortify his camp, immediately commenced operations. Along the brow of the river hills he threw up a line of breast-works about three fourths of a mile in extent, with a strong battery at each extremity, and one in or near the centre, in such positions as to sweep the flats intervening between them and the river. From the foot of the hills, across the flats to the river, an entrenchment was opened, at the extremity of which, on the margin of the river, was constructed another strong battery; and another breast-work and battery a little in advance of the last, and near where the road crossed Mill creek, the bridge having been broken up. These were the principal, and I may say, the only fortifications completed, previous to the action on the nineteenth of September. The engineer having the direction of the American works at Bemis's Heights, was the celebrated Polish patriot, Thaddeus Kosciusko, who had also served in the same capacity at Ticonderoga.

This celebrated engineer came to this country utterly unprovided with letters of recommendation, or introduction, and nearly penniless, and offered himself as a volunteer in the American cause, and solicited an interview with General Washington. "What do you seek here?" inquired the General with his accustomed brevity. "I come to fight as a volunteer for American Independence," was the equally brief and fearless reply. "What can you do?" was Washington's next question; to which Kosciusko, with his characteristic simplicity, only rejoined, "Try me." This was done; occasion soon offered, in which his talents, science and valor were evinced, and above all his great character was duly appreciated. He was speedily made an officer, and further distinguished himself.

He had not been long in America, when he had occasion to display his undaunted courage, as a captain of a company of volunteers. Generals Wayne and Lafayette, notwithstanding the heat of the battle in which they themselves were fully engaged, observed with satisfaction the exertions of that company, which advanced beyond all the rest, and made its attack in the best order.

"Who led the first company?" asked Lafayette of his comrades, on the morning on that memorable day, the 30th of September.

The answer was, "It is a young Pole, of noble birth, but very poor; his name if I am not mistaken, is Kosciusko." The sound of this unusual name, which he could hardly pronounce, filled the French hero with so eager a desire for the brave stranger's acquaintance that he ordered his horse to be immediately saddled, and rode to the village about two miles off, where the volunteers were quartered for the night.

Who shall describe the pleasure of the one, or the surprise of the other, when the General, entering the tent, saw the captain, still covered from head to foot with blood, dust, and sweat, seated at a table, his head resting upon his hand, a map of the country spread out before him, and pen and ink by his side. A cordial grasp of the hand imparted to the modest hero his commander's satisfaction, and the object of a visit paid at so unusual an hour. Kosciusko was appointed an engineer, with the rank of colonel, in October, 1776. After fortifying the camp of General Gates, he was sent to West Point to erect the works there. He was highly esteemed both by American and French officers. At the close of the Revolutionary war, he returned to his native country, and was made Major-General under Poniatowski. In the latter part of his life, having no country of his own, he retired to Switzerland, where he died, Oct. 16th, 1817.

During the time (near a month) that Burgoyne, with his army, lay at and near Battenkill, an incident took place, which I think worthy of notice, as showing the spirit and ardor of the Whigs, in those troublous times; and their determination to cut off all supplies from the invading army.

The Tories, or Cowboys, as they were then

called, were in the constant habit of plundering the inhabitants on both sides of the river, of their grain, poultry, and other kinds of eatables, and driving off their cattle, hogs, and sheep, whenever they could find them, for the purpose of supplying the British army with provisions, for which no doubt they were well paid. Though often pursued, and sometimes roughly handled by the Whigs, they still persisted. At one time in particular, they had collected and secreted in a deep dark ravine, branching off from Mill creek, a large quantity of provisions, such as beef, pork, flour, and other articles of consumption, with the intention of transporting them, at some favorable opportunity, to the British camp. By accident it was found out, and the place of concealment discovered; upon which my father, at the head of about twenty resolute fellows, which he had collected together and well armed, went on in the night, for the purpose of taking or destroying their plunder. On their arrival within a short distance of the depot, one of them crept slily along, when he discovered the Tories, about thirty in number; five of whom appeared to be armed and keeping guard, while the others were in the act of loading four waggons which stood a short distance from the depot, and which they had brought for the purpose of conveying away their stores. The assailing party then held a secret council of war, to consult whether, the enemy being so much superior in number, it was advisable to proceed; whereupon it was unanimously agreed that they should "go ahead," and made their arrangements accordingly.

The place where the stores were concealed, was behind a point projecting from the opposite side, around which the ravine curved, forming the bank on the side of the assailants into a semicircle, around which, it was preconcerted, they should extend themselves in couples, and silently approach the bank or brow of the hill, and at the word of command, *"Come on, boys!"* they were all to give a whoop, and rush on, though not to fire unless the Tories made resistance; but in that case, to fight their way through in the best way they could. All preliminaries being arranged, they formed themselves in order of battle, and silently moved on to the brow of the hill forming the ravine; and when my father, who was at the head, and as previously agreed, gave the word, "Come on boys!" they gave such horrid, continued, and frightful yells, and at the same time rushing down the hill like a mighty torrent, that by the time they had got to the bottom of the ravine, the enemy had all decamped, leaving their arms and baggage a prey to the victors. The assailants not yet satisfied, pursued on a considerable distance, shouting, whooping, and making the woods ring with their horrid yells, as though a thousand Indians had been let loose upon the frightened fugitives. Having found no enemy in their pursuit, the assailants returned to the deserted camp, to examine their booty; but as the Tories had not yet brought, or had concealed their horses, and having no means of bringing off the wagons, they went to work and broke them in pieces, as much as they could. Having stove in the barrels, and scattered and otherwise destroyed the flour and other provisions, they all returned home safe and sound, and much to the joy and gratification of their families and friends; bringing with them twenty-five stand of arms, with which Burgoyne had furnished the Tories, and which the victors considered lawful prize.

Thus ended this hazardous and praiseworthy exploit, and for which my father was honored

with the title of *captain,* a title, as is now well
known to many, by which, for a number of
years, he was addressed, and until he was appointed a civil magistrate, when the title was
exchanged for *esquire.*

About the same time, small parties of Indians were seen prowling about the vicinity,
of whom my father and a few resolute fellows
had been in pursuit. On their return, he had
occasion, while the others passed on, to call at
a Mr. Ezekiel Ensign's, who afterwards, and
for a number of years, kept a public house a
little north of Wilber's Basin. While sitting
there about nine o'clock in the evening, in conversation with Mr. Ensign, a ferocious looking
giant-like Indian, armed and accoutred in the
usual costume of an aboriginal warrior, ushered
himself into the room, and after eyeing them
sharply for a moment, he with one hand drew
from his belt a huge tomahawk, which he
flourished about his head in true Indian style,
and with the other a long scalping-knife, whose
glittering steel became more brilliant in the
dazzling glare of a bright torch-light, and with
which he exhibited, in pantomime, his dexterous manner of taking scalps. At the same
time, with eyes flashing fire, and turning al-

ternately from one to the other, as they sat in opposite directions, he accompanied his daring acts, in broken English, with threats of instant death, if they attempted to move or speak. Ensign being a cripple in one arm, having at some former time accidentally received a charge of shot through his shoulder, and feeling his own weakness, should resistance become necessary, and being in momentary expectation of receiving the fatal blow, he became fixed and inmovable in his chair, with a countenance of ashy paleness,

Obstupuit, steteruntque comæ, et vox faucibus hæsit.

On the other hand, my father, being a man of great muscular strength, and of uncommon agility, and having had many encounters with the Indians, for which they owed him a grudge, prepared himself, with much presence of mind, for a desperate event. To this effect, while the Indian, in his threatening manner, would momentarily direct his attention to Ensign, he would, imperceptibly and by degrees, turn himself in his chair, and in this manner would from time to time, keep silently moving by little and little, until he succeeded in placing himself in a position in which he could grasp with both hands, the back posts of his chair. Thus situated, and knowing the lives of both of them depended altogether on his own exertions, he watched his opportunity, and the moment the Indian turned his eye from him, he grasped the chair, and with almost the rapidity of lightning, sprang upon his feet, whirled the chair over his head, and aimed at him a desperate blow: but the chair raking the ceiling above, and the Indian at the same time, and almost as quick as thought, dodging the blow, he missed his aim. The Indian, having recovered his position, immediately sprang, with a hideous yell, and with his tomahawk uplifted, ready to strike the fatal blow; but before he could effect his direful purpose, the chair was brought around the second time, and with redoubled force, athwart his head and shoulders, which brought him to the floor.

No sooner had he fallen, than my father, dropping his chair, sprang upon him, and wrenched from his firm grasp, the dreadful weapons of death; and would have disabled him on the spot, but Ensign, who by this time had recovered the power of speech, and supposing he intended to take the Indian's life, begged of him not to kill him in the house.

He then holding him in his firm grasp, called for a rope, which was soon procured, and with the assistance of Ensign, he succeeded, though not without a dreadful struggle, in binding the savage monster. By this time, two of the neighbors who had been alarmed by some female of the family, came in, when he was shut up in an out-house, with the doors barred and left in their keeping during the remainder of the night; to be disposed of in the morning as circumstances might require. In the night, the guard believing him secure, and allowing themselves to fall asleep, he made his escape, by removing some portion of the floor and under wall, on the opposite side of the prison to which his guard was posted, much to the regret, not only of his victor, but to many of the neighbors, who had flocked together to obtain a sight of the *conquered savage.*

At another time seven of those maurauding Tories, who had distinguished themselves by a series of desperate acts not to be patiently endured by the community, were taken prisoners, conveyed to Albany, and confined in the city prison, since known as the old museum, and from which they once made their escape, but only to enjoy their liberty a few hours, for they were soon retaken and condemned to the gallows. The public indignation was much excited by their conduct in prison, and the circumstances attending their being brought to suffer the sentence of the law. They were confined in the right hand room of the lower story of the prison. The door of their apartment swung in a place cut out lower than the level of the floor. When the sheriff came to take them out he found the door barricaded. He procured a heavy piece of timber with which he in vain endeavored to batter down the door, although he was assisted in the operation by some very athletic and willing individuals. During the attempt, the voices of the prisoners were heard threatening death to those who persevered in the attempt, with the assertion that they had a train of powder to blow up themselves and their assailants. Indeed it was well ascertained, that a quantity of powder had passed into their possession, but how, could not be known. It was afterwards found placed under the floor, and arranged to produce the threatened result. The sheriff could not effect his entrance, while a crowd of gazers looked on to see the end of this singular contest. Some one suggested the idea of getting to them through the ceiling, and immediately went to work to effect a passage, by cutting a hole through. While this was going on, the prisoners renewed their threats, with vows of vengeance speedy, awful and certain. The assailants, however, persevered, and having procured a fire-engine, placed it so as to introduce the hose suddenly to the hole in the ceiling, and at a given signal inundated the room beneath. This was dexterously performed. The powder and its train were in an instant rendered useless. Still, however, to descend was the difficulty, as but one person could do so at a time. The disproportion of physical strength that apparently awaited the first intruder, prevented, for some time, any further attempt. At last an Irishman, by the name of McDole, who was a merchant, exclaimed, "give me an Irishman's gun, and I will go first!" He was instantly provided with a formidable cudgel, and with this in his hand he descended, and at the same moment in which he struck the floor, he leveled the prisoner near him, and continued to lay about him violently until the room was filled with a strong party of citizens, who came to his assistance through the hole in the ceiling. After a hard struggle they were secured and the door which had been barricaded by brick taken from the fireplace, was opened.

They were almost immediately taken out for execution, and the mob was sufficiently exasperated to have instantly taken their punishment into their own hands. The prisoners while moving up the hill to the place of execution, wore an air of great gloom and ill nature. No one appeared to pity them, and their own hopes of being released by some fortunate circumstance, as by the intervention of the enemy, had now vanished forever.

Having arrived at the summit of the hill, near, or at the very place now covered with elegant and substantial edifices, north and east of the academy, they there, upon one gallows of rude construction, ended their miserable lives together.

The transaction created considerable excitement, and was considered by the Tories as a cruel and unnecessary waste of life, and a sacrifice to the unnatural feelings which had dictated the unhappy rebellion. By the Whigs, it was considered as a necessary example, demanded by the nature of the times and the enormity of the offences they had committed, and they considered it not only a justifiable, but an imperious act of necessity, to inflict upon the offenders the full penalties of the law.

CHAPTER VI

Burgoyne, having used the most unremitting industry and perseverance in bringing stores forward from Fort George, and having at length, by strenuous efforts, obtained about thirty days' provisions, formed the resolution of passing the Hudson with his army in order to engage the Americans, and force a passage to Albany.*

---

*Albany has been memorable in American history. It was the rendezvous, and the point of departure, for most of these armies, which, whether sent by the mother country, or raised by the colonies themselves, for the conquest of the Gallo-American dominions, and of the savages, so often during the middle periods of the last century, excited, and more than once disappointed the hopes of the empire. It was scarcely less conspicuous in the same manner, during the war of the Revolution, and during the late war with Great Britain. Few places on this side of the Atlantic, have seen more of martial array, or heard more frequently the dreadful note of preparation. Still, (except perhaps in some of the

BURGOYNE'S CAMPAIGN

As a swell of the water, occasioned by great rains had carried away his bridge of rafts, he constructed another of boats, over the river at a shoal place of the water, just above the mouth of Battenkill. And in order to cross, he encamped on an extensive flat or interval, about one hundred rods north of Lansing's saw-mill. The farm, till within a few years, was occupied by Mr. Thomas Rogers. Burgoyne had quite an extensive slaughter yard there, which so enriched the soil, that its effects are still visible on the corn crops and other productions. On the bank of the river where the army made their flotilla to cross

---

early contests, with the Aborigines) it has never seen an enemy; a hostile army has never encamped before it; nor have its women and children ever seen the smoke of an enemy's camp.

More than once, however, has a foreign enemy, after fixing his determination for Albany, been either arrested, and turned back in his career, or visited the desired spot in captivity and disgrace.

The French invasions from Canada, never came nearer than Schenectady. In 1777, the portentous advances of the British armies from the same place, and of the British fleets and armies, from New-York, threatening a junction at Albany, and filling the new states with alarm, and the Cabinet of St. James with premature exultations, met a most signal discomfiture.

with their cannon, &c. they threw up an embankment, about twenty rods in extent, running parallel with the river, and mounted with several pieces of cannon, to protect the army in case of opposition, while crossing. The remains of this bank are still visible, and are mostly covered with brush wood, which skirts the bank of the river. On the thirteenth and fourteenth of September, he crossed with his army here, and at a shoal one mile below, to the right bank of the Hudson, and encamped on the heights of Saratoga, (Schuylerville.) On the fifteenth, having succeeded in getting his artilley and baggage all across, he moved down as far as Do-ve-gat, (Coveville) where he halted two days, for the purpose of repairing the roads and bridges in his advance, for the more convenient march of his army. On the seventeenth he advanced as far as the "Sword-house," about two miles above John Taylor's, (which has been mistaken by many for the "Sword-house,") where he encamped for the night. On this day, Gen. Arnold, with about fifteen hundred men, was sent out to harass him and impede his progress; but the country at that time was so thickly wooded, and the land along the river hills and their vicinity, so cut up with deep and almost impassable ravines, as to render it impracticable to attack him in flank, and to attack so powerful an army in front would not have been advisable; consequently he returned without accomplishing anything, excepting some slight skirmishing with the British advance guard.

On the eighteenth Burgoyne continued his march as far as what is now called "Wilber's Basin,"* at the northern extremity of the alluvial flats, before mentioned, and within about two miles of the American camp. Here he fortified his camp, with breast works and redoubts, in a line extending from the river to a range of hills about forty rods distant, and

---

* Northeast of the American camp, and about five miles distant, is quite an elevated portion of land called "Willard's Mountain," from the following fact. At the time Burgoyne, with his veteran army, was encamped at and near Wilber's Basin, a man by the name of Willard, in company with a few others, took a good spy-glass, and went to the top of this mountain, for the purpose of ascertaining, as near as possible, the number of the British troops, the situation of their camp, and to watch their movements, and made his reports accordingly; which, it was said, were of much benefit to the Americans, and from which circumstances, it has ever since retained the appellation of "Willard's Mountain."

upon which, and the plain in the rear, was posted the division under General Frazer, and upon the very ground, beneath the surface of which, the bones of that gallant officer are now mouldering into dust.

At this time the American army were disposed in the following order; the main body, composing the right wing, and under the immediate command of General Gates, occupied the river hills, and the defile between those and the river; the left wing, under General Arnold, and composed of General Poor's brigade, Morgan's rifle regiment and a portion of the militia, were posted on the Heights about three-fourths of a mile in rear of the river hills; and General Learned, with his brigade and two regiments of militia, occupied the plain or centre.

Thus circumstanced, the nineteenth of September was reserved by destiny for an obstinate and sanguinary action, in which it was at length to be decided whether the Americans, as some pretended, could only resist the English when protected by the strength of works, or of woods, rivers and mountains, or if they were capable of meeting them upon equal ground, in fair and regular battle.

About ten o'clock, the British troops formed themselves in order of march, with a full determination of forcing their way through the American lines, and made their arrangements accordingly. Burgoyne's intention, as was afterwards authentically ascertained, with the center division, of which he took command in person, and the right wing under General Frazer, was by a circuitous route, to concentrate their forces at the head of the middle ravine near the left wing of the Americans; turn that wing, and fall upon the rear of the American camp; at the same time a strong force composing the left wing, and artillery under Generals Phillips and Reidesel, were to move along the main road near the margin of the river, to within about half a mile of the American lines; and at a given signal, make an attack in front and force their way through. And in order to keep up a perfect understanding between the divisions under Burgoyne and Frazer, and that composing the left wing, three minute guns were to be fired, at the junction of the former, for the latter to advance.

As soon as it was ascertained that Burgoyne was on the advance, and in separate divisions, Arnold, feeling anxious to begin the "game," pressed General Gates with much earnestness to permit him to march out and make the attack in advance of the American lines, and solicited a portion of the troops composing the right wing. Gates at first refused, prefering to await his approach at the entrenchments, and, besides, it was at that moment somewhat uncertain where Burgoyne intended his first attack, consequently he objected to the drawing off any of the forces from the river, as Phillips and Reidesel were already on the march. But Arnold, anticipating Burgoyne's intentions, which afterwards proved correct, and pressing with so much force, the propriety of an attack in advance, as a means of disconcerting his plan of operations, and checking the progress of the left wing of the British army, that General Gates finally yielded, and directed him to send out Colonel Morgan's rifle corps and a portion of the infantry, and to support them himself if necessary; but refused any assistance from the right wing, excepting Colonel Scammell's regiment. It has ever been a matter of surprise, to those who were present at the time, and well acquainted with the facts, that, after Phillips and Reidesel fell back, General Gates did not allow Arnold to draw reinforcements from the right wing, in which case, the victory no doubt would have been complete.

It has been stated by almost all who have written upon the subject, and even by Wilkinson, of whom I may have occasion to speak hereafter, that the battle of the nineteenth of September was *accidental* in its commencement. It is true it may have been accidental on the part of Burgoyne, inasmuch as he did not expect the Americans would meet and attack him where they did; but in the sense in which the idea of *accidence* appears intended to be conveyed, it never has been understood by those who were present and well acquainted with the facts, and had honesty enough to relate them in all their truth and simplicity. If the attack was not intended by Burgoyne, as above stated, with due deference, I would ask, why did the left wing move down the river to within half a mile of the American lines? and why were those signal guns to be fired on the junction of the two divisions under Burgoyne and Frazer? and why did their baggage remain on board of their boats and other conveyances, all of which are well known and incontestible facts? These are questions of moment, and ought to be satisfactorily answered by those who assert the action to have been accidental in its commencement.

But to resume. Burgoyne, with the center division, followed the course of the stream now forming Wilber's basin, about half a mile, then struck off in nearly a southwest direction, and through some partial clearings, until he arrived a little south of what was then called "Freeman's Cottage;" his front and flanks being covered by Indians, Provincials, and Canadians. The division composing the right wing, under General Frazer, took a circuitous route along a new road partially opened, leading from the river and intersecting the road from Bemis's Heights, north, about two and a half miles from the American camp; and from this place of intersection, proceeded south towards the American left, until they arrived at some high ground about one hundred and fifty rods west of Freeman's Cottage. At this moment, Colonel Morgan, who had been detached to observe the movements of the British, and to harrass them as they advanced, fell in with the Canadians and Indians, in advance of Burgoyne, at the middle ravine south of Freeman's Cottage, where he attacked them sharply, and drove them back till they were reinforced by a strong corps, under Major Forbes, about midway between the ravine and cottage, where a brisk engagement took place; but the British were finally driven back to their line which was then forming, in an open wood in rear of the cottage, where they were again reinforced, and Morgan in turn compelled to retire. Major Dearborn, with a battallion of light infantry, being ordered to the assistance of Morgan, whose riflemen had been considerably scattered by the vigor of the attack, the battle was renewed about one o'clock. About this time, Arnold, with his command, consisting of a part of Learned's brigade and of the New-York troops, appeared on the field, and made an attempt to cut off Frazer, who was now rapidly advancing, from the center division or main body under Burgoyne. But Frazer was, at the same time, endeavoring to execute a similar movement upon him, while neither of them was able, on account of the woods, to perceive the movements of his enemy. The two parties met about sixty rods west of the cottage, on a plain or level piece of ground. Arnold exhibited on this occasion all the impetuosity of his courage; he encouraged his men with voice and example. The action soon became warm, close, and bloody; the enemy, fearing that Arnold, by cutting their line, would penetrate between the right wing and center division, as was manifestly his intention, hastened with two regiments of infantry and Breyman's riflemen, to reinforce the point attacked; who poured so galling a fire into the right flank of the Americans, that, after contesting the ground inch by inch for more than an hour, they finally broke and gave way, when Arnold was compelled to retire and resume his place in the line.

The principal scene of the subsequent action, was on what was then called Freeman's Farm,* of which the following is a description of the ground. In front of Freeman's cottage

---

* "Freeman's Cottage," or "Freeman's Farm," as it was then called, lies about half a mile east of the road leading to the Quaker Springs, and is now occupied by the widow and heirs of William Leggett, deceased. A farm now owned by

was an oblong clearing, skirted by an open wood, about sixty rods in length from east to west, containing twelve or fifteen acres, and sloping to the east and south.

About three o'clock in the afternoon, both armies were drawn up in a line of battle; the British, consisting of the 9th, 21st, 62d and 20th regiments of Hamilton's brigade, and Jones's corps of grenadiers and artillery, on the north, and the Americans on the south of this clearing. Burgoyne being now at the head of his army, and the Americans having been reinforced by four regiments under Lieutenant-Colonels Brooks, Cilley and Scammel, and Majors Dearborn and Hull, the action commenced, and soon became general, and the combatants evinced that ardor and gallantry which showed a determination to conquer or die. Such was now the valor and impetuosity of the Americans, which continued without intermission for more than an hour, that the British troops began to fall into con-

---

the heirs of Isaac Freeman, deceased, and immediately between the foregoing and the said road, then occupied by George Coulter, is often mistaken for the "Freeman Farm" above alluded to.

fusion; but General Phillips soon appeared with fresh men and a part of the artillery. Upon hearing the firing, he had rapidly made his way up the river hills, and through a very difficult wood to the scene of danger, and restored the action at the very moment it was about to be decided in favor of the Americans. The Americans being again reinforced by Gen. Learned's brigade, the firing, for about three hours, was incessant, with continued and tremendous roar and blaze, filling the field with carnage and death. Few battles have been more obstinate and unyielding—at one point the British are overpowered; but being reinforced, the Americans are baffled: these, being supported and renewing their efforts, regain their advantages; the same ground is occupied alternately; the dead and wounded are now promiscuously mingled together; the British resort repeatedly to their bayonets, without effect; the Americans resist and foil their attempts.

Major Jones of the British artillery, had the command of four pieces of cannon, which he conducted with great skill and valor till he fell, and thirty-six out of forty-eight of his artillerymen were either killed or wounded; his cannon were repeatedly taken and retaken, but finally remained with the enemy for want of horses to bring them off. The sixty-second regiment, under Colonel Anstruther, of Hamilton's brigade, was also literally cut to pieces; after the action is did not exceed sixty men, and five or six officers, fit for duty. The Colonel and his Major, Harnage, were wounded. During the engagement a number of the Americans placed themselves in the boughs of high trees, in the rear and flanks, and took every opportunity of destroying the British officers by single shot; and in this way Captain Green, aid of General Phillips, was shot through the arm, at a moment when he happened to pass between the ball and General Burgoyne, at whom it was aimed.

In the dusk of the evening the battle terminated, the British in one quarter silently retreated, the Americans in another gave way and quit the long contested field. Lieutenant-Colonel Brooks, who with the eighth Massachusetts regiment, was engaged with Breyman's riflemen, remained on the field till about eleven o'clock at night, and was the last who returned. So engaged were the Americans, that many of them, after having their wounds dressed, returned again to the fight.

Major Hull commanded a detachment of about two hundred men, who fought with such signal ardor, that more than half of them were either killed or wounded; and during the heat of the action, a party of the British having stationed themselves in and near the cottage, from which they were making havoc among his men, he detached a band of brave fellows for the purpose, who made a rush, drove them with much slaughter from their position, and took their cannon; and all in less time than it takes to record the fact.

Towards the close of the day, General Learned's brigade, and one other regiment, I think Marshall's, were principally engaged on a rise of ground west of the cottage, with the British grenadiers and a regiment of British infantry, and bravely contested the ground till

Put 'n end to the conflict. A scene now of horror
Was open'd to view on the dawn of the morrow;
For on parts of the field where the battle most rag'd,
Lay Britons and Yankees, both the young and the ag'd
Promisc'ously mingled—about forty-two score,
Of the dying and dead lay weltering in gore!

night, which has so often and so kindly interposed to stop the carnage of contending hosts,

Both parties claimed the victory. The English, it is true kept possession of the field; yet, as the intention of the Americans was, not to advance, but to maintain their position, and that of the English not to maintain theirs, but to gain ground, and as besides, it was a victory for the Americans not to be vanquished, it is easy to see which had the advantage, of the day. On the other hand, the English were now convinced, to the great prejudice of their hopes, and even of their courage, that they would have to grapple with a foe as eager for action, as careless of danger, and as indifferent with respect to ground or cover, as themselves.

The whole number of Americans engaged in this battle, was about three thousand; the remainder of the army, from its unfavorable situation, being near the river, and for reasons before stated, took no part in the action.

About three thousand five hundred of the British were engaged, more than five hundred of whom, were either killed, wounded, or taken prisoners. On the side of the Americans three hundred and fifteen were killed, wounded, or missing. Among the killed were Lieutenant-Colonels Adams and Colburn, of Poor's brigade, both able and efficient officers.

At the same time the left wing of the British army was moving down the river, a party of Canadians, Loyalists, and Savages were detached through the skirt of the woods along the margin of the flats, where, at that time, was a bye road, traveled only in time of great freshets, the flats at such time being overflowed. General Gates, having received information of their approach, detached about three hundred men to intercept them; they were met on a flat piece of ground bordering on Mill creek, where a smart skirmish took place, which lasted, with much obstinacy on both sides, about twenty minutes, when the enemy being much cut up and broken, finally gave way and fled in every direction; leaving thirteen dead on the field, and thirty-five taken prisoners.

This was the first action, fought with any portion of Burgoyne's army after he crossed the river; being terminated about the same time that Morgan commenced the action near the Heights.

I have, within a few years, been informed by a Mr. Hoose, who was in the action, that the enemy, being reinforced, rallied again, and drove the Americans within their entrenchments, where about one hundred followed, who, a reinforcement at that moment arriving, were immediately surrounded and every man taken prisoner; and the remainder, after a sharp contest for about fifteen minutes, were compelled to flee.

From some of the prisoners taken in this skirmish, General Gates received the first certain information of Burgoyne's intention of trying to force a passage through the American lines, and of his manner of attack; which determined him to keep a strong force on the flats and river hills.

The next day, Arnold being anxious to renew the attack, was opposed by Gen. Gates, and possibly for the following reasons. At the close of the preceding battle, such was the difficulty at that time of procuring ammunition, that the American soldiers composing the left wing, and who had been engaged, had not a second round of cartridges left, nor were they to be procured at the magazine; a fact not made known to any of the officers excepting General Gates, until after a supply had been obtained from Albany, when the secret was first disclosed. Upon which Arnold, feeling a deep sense of the deplorable situation in which the army would have been placed, had the action been renewed the next day by the British troops, as they were in hourly expectation; very politely asked General Gates why he had not made the fact known to him. Gates replied in his usual gruff manner, "It was bad enough for me to know it myself."

About the time General Phillips arrived on the field with the artillery, General Arnold, on a grey horse, and under full speed from the scene of action, rode up to General Gates, who was on the Heights at the time, sitting upon his horse, and listening to the tremendous firing, and addressed him in the following laconic manner: "General, the British are reinforced; we must have more men." General Gates immediately replied, "You shall have them, sir," and immediately ordered out General Learned's brigade; when Arnold again hurried back on a full gallop, and the men after him in double quick time.

These incidents, which were well known at the time, and often spoken of afterwards, even up to this day, the author relates in corroboration of the facts stated by him, in contradiction to what has been said by General Wilkinson respecting Arnold. I have somewhere seen it stated by Wilkinson, that during this action, Generals Gates and Arnold sat on their horses near the *center* of the American camp, listening to the firing, while he, (Wilkinson) I think, was much on the field, directing the movements of the American forces. But those acquainted with the situation of the country at that time; the dense forest that intervened between the center of the camp and the battle field; its more remote situation, and consequently from its position, there was more difficulty in hearing; and also knowing the relative situation of the Heights on the left, where Arnold's division was posted, and where the attack was intended, by Burgoyne, to have been made, and the open ground intervening between those Heights and the field of action: I feel confident, were there nothing else to confute it, that they would, at once, see the fallacy of Wilkinson's statement: and I also think that Colonel Stone, had he known the situation of the whole ground, and the circumstances of this battle, would not have set down Wilkinson's account of it as the best that has been written. It is possible, however, that Wilkinson's account of any transaction where Arnold was not concerned, may be as correct as any extant.

Whether these errors were intentionally committed by Wilkinson, or whether *he* was intoxicated at the time; or finally, whether he was so blinded by *jealousy,* a feeling, which, it was well known at that time, existed towards Arnold, was the cause of those errors, I will leave for the reader to inquire; while I deem it sufficient for me to point them out, and correct them, by such facts and circumstances as have come to my knowledge. Not that I would, by any means, attempt to justify the after and traitorous conduct of Arnold, for on one can more highly condemn that unfortunate step, than I do myself, nor can I suppose any possible circumstances that would justify him in taking the course that he did; but at the same time, as my object is to "nothing extenuate or aught set down in malice," I am therefore willing to give "honor to whom honor is due," and it has been the common belief, especially in this part of the Union, that one cause of his turning a traitor as he did, was in consequence of his not having received due credit for his management and gallantry in and during the truly "memorable battles on Bemis's Heights." It is perhaps difficult to speak of the deeds of such a man as Arnold, without remembering the deplorable issue to which he was finally brought, by his folly and wickedness; yet the historian should never forget that he commits a crime little less flagrant in its nature, if inferior in its magnitude, when he allows himself to be so far moved by his feelings, as to depart from the strict line of truth and justice, or, by such an obliquity, to lead his readers to form a false and harsh judgment.

A serious misunderstanding arose about this time between Gates and Arnold, which is supposed to have been owing to the officious interference of Wilkinson, who was adjutant-general to the army, and who insisted on the returns of a part of Arnold's division being made to him, and influenced Gates to sustain his demand; which was done in general orders, without giving notice to Arnold. And in his official communication to congress, respecting the battle, General Gates said nothing of Arnold or his division, but merely stated that the action was fought by detachments from the *army*. Arnold complained of this neglect as ungenerous, not more in regard to himself than to the troops under his immediate command. A sharp correspondence ensued, and Arnold was finally deprived of his command.

There is room to believe that a spice of jealousy was also mingled with Gates's feelings at that time. Colonel Varick, military secretary to General Schuyler, in writing from camp to that officer three days after the action, said, "He seems to be piqued, that Arnold's division had the honor of beating the enemy on the 19th. This I am certain of, that Arnold has all the credit of the action." And after the convention of Saratoga, Colonel Varick again wrote as follows in a letter from Albany. "During Burgoyne's stay here, he gave Arnold great credit for his *bravery* and military abilities, especially in the action of the 19th, whenever he spoke of him, and once in the presence of General Gates." He certainly, I think, could not have referred to his *bravery* in sitting on his horse, near a mile in rear of the field of battle, and secreted behind a dense intervening forest, where Wilkinson has very erroneously placed him. The fact of Arnold's being on the field during the action of the 19th, and actually heading the troops that engaged Frazer's division, is also confirmed by a number who were present, and many of whom were engaged in that battle.

With these few remarks I will leave Wilkinson, with all his errors, in the hands of the reader, to be dealt with as he may think most advisable, while I myself am proceeding on and preparing the way for an account of a more decisive battle.

CHAPTER VII

The day following the action, General Burgoyne, finding that he must abandon all idea of dislodging the Americans by force, from their entrenched positions, endeavored to console himself with the hope, that time might offer him some occasion, to operate with more effect.

Resolving, therefore, to pause, he pitched his camp within cannon shot of the American lines. He threw up a line of entrenchments, with batteries, across the plain to the river hills; also an entrenchment with batteries, across the defile at the northern extremity of

the flats, and extending to the river on his left,
the whole being about two miles in extent. An
English regiment, the Hessians of Hanau, and
a detachment of Loyalists were encamped on
the flats, where he had established his magazines and hospitals, for greater security.

While these preparations were going on at
the British camp, the Americans were not idle.
They now extended and completed their line
of breastworks, from the north-eastern angle
on the river hills, west, across the farm then
owned by the late John Neilson, Esq., deceased,
about three-fourths of a mile, to the Heights
on the left, and to within a few rods of his
dwelling house now occupied by his son the
present writer. From the Heights on the left,
and a few rods north of the dwelling house,
the entrenchments extended south and southwest, about three-fourths of a mile, to a great
ravine. At the northwest angle stood a large
log barn, which was strengthened by a double
tier of logs on three sides, and strong batteries, in circular form, extending from each extremity, south, about one hundred and fifty
feet, and encircled by a deep trench and palisades or pickets; the whole area within the
circle of the pockets, was near half an acre,

and out of respect to the owner, who was a very active Whig, it was honored with the name of Fort Neilson. A little left of the center, between the northern extremities, was a strong battery, and also about fifty rods south of the fort was another; and in the rear, near the center of the encampment, was their magazine, which was also fortified. Much of these fortifications are still existing; sufficient to plainly trace their line, and the positions of the several batteries. The front of the camp was covered from the right to the left by a deep ravine, running nearly parallel with the line, and a great part of the way by a dense forest. From a little left of the fort and for some distance west, large trees were felled in every direction, which presented an almost insurmountable barrier.

Thus fortified, General Gates, having given up the command of the right wing to General Lincoln, assumed that of the left, and moved his head quarters from Bemis's house near the river, to a house standing about one hundred rods south of the fort, and owned by Captain Ephraim Woodworth; the left being composed of two brigades under Generals Poor and Learned, Colonel Morgan's rifle corps, and a part of the New England Militia: Colonel Morgan occupying the Heights immediately south of the fort, General Learned's brigade, the plain below or on the east, and General Poor's brigade, the Heights south of Morgan, and between him and General Gates's head quarters.

The British troops were disposed in the following order: the Hessians under Colonel Breyman occupied the extreme right, or right flank defence, the light infantry, under Lord Balcarras, and Frazer's elite, that part of the camp around Freeman's cottage, flanked by the grenadiers and Hamilton's brigade, on their left, and extending to the north branch ravine. The remainder of the army, including Reidesel's command, occupied the plain, and the ground north of Wilber's Basin, to protect their magazine and hospital.

Thus the two armies lay, in lines parallel to each other, and within cannon shot distance, from the nineteenth of September until the seventh of October; though not without great anxiety on both sides; and scarcely a night passed without firing, and sometimes concerted attacks upon the British pickets; no foraging party could be made without great detachments to cover them; it was the plan of the Americans to harrass the British army by constant alarms, and their superiority of numbers now enabled them to attempt it, without fatigue to themselves. It has been said, and no doubt truly, that neither officer nor soldier of the British army, ever slept during that interval, without his clothes, or that any general officer or commander of a regiment, passed a single night without being upon his legs occasionally, at different hours, and constantly an hour before daylight.

At one time while the two armies were thus encamped near each other, about twenty of the most resolute inhabitants in the vicinity, collected together for the purpose of having a frolic, as they termed it, of some kind or other. After their arrival at the place of rendezvous, and a number of propositions had been logically discussed, they finally concluded, with more courage than prudence, that, by a *coup-demain*, they would go and bring in one of the British advance pickets, which was posted on the north bank of the middle ravine. Having, with much formality, selected their several officers, and furnished themselves with suitable arms, and other equipments, they marched off in *ir*-regular military style. The martial costume of the Captain, for by such title he was addressed, exhibited the extremes of continental etiquette, personified in one instance, by a sharp and huge three cocked hat, profusely trimmed with the threadbare fragments of thrown-off gold lace, surmounting a well pomatumed and powdered head. A long waisted blue coat, turned up with rather sun-bleached buff, that met and parted at the same time on his breast; a black silk neck-kerchief drawn tightly around his throat, discovering the balance of power, or rather the center of gravity, to be lying some where in the region of the olfactory organ, completed the upper half of this mischief-bent volunteer officer. A pair of buckskin small clothes drawn tightly over a muscular thigh, were met at the knee by a pair of straight-sided boots, that, doubtless, by their stiffness and want of pliability prevented any thing like an attack upon the limb inside. An old white belt thrown over the whole man, and a heavy sabre with a leather scabbard, completed the brilliant costume of this son of chivalry, and *ir*-regular friend of the continental congress.

The other *com*-missioned officers, for such

by way of distinguishment, were they called, were fully armed and accoutred in a similar manner, but somewhat inferior in brilliancy.

Brown tow shirts were the panoply of the *farmer*-soldiers; over their broad shoulders hung powder horns and shot bags, manufactured during the long winter evenings, and now and then stopped up with a corn cob, which had escaped the researches of the "swinish multitude." Muskets were rather uncommon among the inhabitants in those days of martial exploit, and in their stead, long fowling-pieces were substituted.

In such a group of combatants just escaped, as it were, from the tomahawk, hastily equipt for the present emergency, and bearing a grotesque appearance, the name of Steuben was of no more weight than the feather that danced in the breeze. Thus armed and accoutred, these sons of daring interpidity, marched off about ten o'clock at night, with more courage than order, fully determined to conquer or die in the glorious cause of their beloved country, then bleeding at every pore.

As they approached within musket-shot distance of their unsuspecting enemy, they were formed, or rather formed themselves in order of battle, and advanced in three *grand* divisions—one by a circuitous route, to gain their rear, while the other two posted themselves on their flanks. After giving time for each party to gain their several positions, the resolute captain, who was prepared for the purpose, gave the preconcerted signal, by a deafening blast on an old horse trumpet, whose martial sound had often cheered the mounted troops to fierce and bloody combat, when all, with fearless step "rushed bravely on" with clattering arms, through rustling leaves and crackling brush, with the usual parade of a hundred men. As they closed in, the leaders of each division, in a bold and commanding voice, and before the guard could say "Who comes there?" called, or rather bawled out, "Ground your arms, or you are all dead men!" Supposing they were surrounded by a much superior force, and deeming resistance, under such circumstances, of no avail, the officer of the guard gave the orders, when their arms were immediately grounded, and thirty British soldiers surrendered themselves "prisoners of war" to only two-thirds of their number, and those undisciplined American farmers.

By the fourth of October the supplies of

Burgoyne's army were so far reduced that the soldiers were placed on short allowance, and his position was in other respects becoming so critical, that hearing nothing from Sir Henry Clinton, for whose co-operation from New-York he had been waiting since the battle of the nineteenth, he therefore sent for Generals Phillips, Reidesel and Frazer, to consult with them on the best measures to be taken.

His project was to attack and again attempt to turn the left wing of the Americans at once; but the other generals judged that it would be dangerous to leave their stores under so feeble a protection as eight hundred men according to the proposition of their commander. A second consultation was held on the fifth, at which General Reidesel positively declared that the situation of the army had become so critical, that they must either attack and force the entrenchments of General Gates, and thus bring about a favorable change of affairs, or recross the Hudson, and retreat upon Fort George.

Frazer approved of the latter suggestion, and Phillips declined giving an opinion. General Burgoyne, to whom the idea of retreating was most unwelcome, having had an *order* promised him if he succeeded in his campaign, declared that he would make, on the seventh, a reconnoisance as near as possible to the left wing of the Americans, with a view of ascertaining whether it could be attacked with any prospect of success. He would afterwards, either attack the Americans, or retreat by the route in rear of Batten kill. This was his final determination, and dispositions were made accordingly.

During this time of dreadful preparation, information was received by deserters and otherwise, that an attack would soon be made by the British, upon the line of the American entrenchments at the Heights, near the head quarters of General Gates, or that a retreat across the Hudson would be attempted. Accordingly, General Fellows with about fifteen hundred men, was detached across the river, and to take post on the heights opposite the Saratoga ford, to watch their movements, and prevent their passage at that place.

In the afternoon of the sixth, an unusual movement was perceived in the British camp, and especially in that part of it which extended across the plain near the river, which, at that time, induced a belief that the army were about to attempt a retreat during the following night; consequently, General Gates augmented his forces near the river, by drawing off a portion of those on the Heights preparatory to a close pursuit, should that be the case. But it afterwards appeared, that Burgoyne was only arranging his troops, preparatory to such subsequent course as might be determined upon the next day.

On the seventh of October, between ten and eleven o'clock, Burgoyne, having committed the guard of his camp upon the high ground, near Freeman's Cottage, to the Brigadier-Generals Hamilton and Speckt, and that of the redoubts and plain near the river, to Brigadier-General Gall, began to move with about fifteen hunded men to the northern extremity of a low ridge of land, about three-fourths of a mile, and a little north of west, from the American camp, where they displayed, formed the line, and sat down in double ranks. General Gates, having received information of their movements, despatched one of his aids to ascertain their position, and if possible their intentions. He proceeded about half a mile to a small rise of ground, (near Asa Chatfield's house,) where he discovered them, about sixty rods in advance, in a wheat field, and foragers in the act of cutting the wheat or standing straw; and several officers mounted on the top of a cabin (Joseph Munger's,) from whence, with their glasses, they were endeavoring to reconnoitre the American left, which was concealed from their view by intervening woods.

Soon after the return of the officer, a party of Canadians and Savages that were scouring the woods on the flank of the British grenadiers as they were marching from camp, fell in with and attacked the American pickets, near the middle ravine, which were driven in, and followed by the grenadiers to within musket shot distance of Gates's line of entrenchments, where a tremendous discharge of cannon and musquetry took place, which was returned with equal intrepidity by the Americans. For about thirty minutes the action at the breast works, a little south of the fort, was maintained with great obstinacy on both sides.

The grenadiers resorted repeatedly to their bayonets, but were as often resisted by the Americans, and foiled in their attempts. For sometime this bloody conflict continued without any apparent advantage on either side, till at length the Americans being reinforced by a part of Morgan's riflemen, the assailants begun to give way, and finally retreated, with much loss, hotly pursued by the Americans to within a short distance of the British line of battle, which was then forming.

A great many balls have since been picked up on both sides of the breast work, and even to this day, they are found in the direction to which they were fired—some of them flattened and other misshaped, evincing that they had come in collision with opposing obstacles. And here is one circumstance, strongly confirming the often repeated saying, "that the Americans, in addition to one musket ball, added two buck shot, by which they done so much execution," they are frequently found on the side of the breast work to which the Americans fired, and not on the other.

About two o'clock in the afternoon, the British line of battle was formed across a newly cultivated piece of ground; their grenadiers, under Major Ackland, and their artillery under Major Williams, occupied a rise of ground on the left, bordering on a wood and covered in front by the head of the middle ravine: their light-infantry under Lord Balcarras, in a southwestern direction, and on their extreme right, and covered by a rail fence; and the center was composed of British and German battalions, under Generals Phillips and Riedsel.

In advance of the right wing, and near J. Munger's, as before mentioned, were stationed about one thousand men, under Gen. Frazer, (five hundred having been withdrawn) intended to fall on the Americans in flank and rear, while the attack should be made in front.

But General Gates, who observed their movements, and instantly penetrating the design of the British general, directed Col. Morgan with his rifle corps, consisting of about fifteen hundred men, by a circuitous route, and under cover of the woods, to take post on some high ground in front and flank of their advanced right, and make the attack there, as soon as the fire should be opened on the British left.

It was concerted, that time should be allowed Col. Morgan to make the proposed circuit, and gain his station on the enemy's right, before the attack should be made on the left; Gen. Poor's brigade, composed of the New-York and New-Hampshire troops, to be supported by a part of Learned's brigade, was ordered for this service, and the attack was commenced at about thirty minutes after two on the front and flank of the British grenadiers. When Gen. Poor had drawn up his men in order of battle, and given them orders not to fire until they commenced rising the hill, there was, for a moment, an awful pause,—each party seemed to bid defiance to his opponent. At length, however, the grenadiers commenced the action by a shower of grape shot and musket balls, which took no other effect than to mar the trees above the heads of the Americans; who "the din of battle now begun," rushed on firing and opening to the right and left, and forming again on the flanks, mowing down the grenadiers at every shot, until they gained the top of the hill, where a close and bloody conflict ensued, which lasted, with tremendous roar and blaze of artillery and small arms, for about thirty minutes, when the commander of the grenadiers, Major Ackland, was badly wounded, being shot through both legs, and the grenadiers being too vigorously pressed, broke and gave way, leaving the ground thickly strewed with their dead and dying. In this dreadful struggle, one field piece was taken and retaken five times, and finally fell into the hands of the

Americans: upon which Col. Cilley, of New-Hampshire, exulting in its capture, immediately mounted, and it being "sworn true to America," was turned and fired on the British troops, with their own ammunition, which was left in the boxes.

Soon after Gen. Poor commenced the attack upon the grenadiers, a flanking party of the British was discovered advancing, by a circuitous route, through the woods; upon which Col. Cilley was ordered with his regiment to intercept them. As he approached near to a brush fence, the British troops rose from behind it, and immediately fired, but did it so hurriedly that only a few balls took effect. The commander of the British, then ordered his men to "Fix bayonets, and charge the d—d rebels." Col. Cilley who heard the order, responded, "It takes two to play at that game—charge, and we will try it!" The Americans charged at the word, and rushing upon the enemy discharged a volley in their faces, when they immediately broke and fled, leaving many of their number dead and wounded on the field.

As soon as the action commenced on the British left, Colonel Morgan, who had posted his men as directed, poured down, unexpectedly, upon the British right advance, and after a sharp contest drove them in with much slaughter; then by a sudden movement to his left, he fell upon the flank of the British right, with such impetuosity, and with a so well directed fire, that they soon fell into confusion; and while attempting to change their front, Major Dearborn, who at that critical moment had arrived on the field with two regiments of New-England troops, poured so galling a fire into their flank and rear, that they soon broke, and were compelled to retire. They were however, again rallied and reformed by the Earl of Balcarras, behind a fence in rear of their first position; but being again attacked in front and flank, with so great vigor by superior numbers, that resistance became vain, and the whole right wing gave way.

While the battle was furiously raging here and at the British left, Arnold, who had become very restless after the action commenced, and who, without orders, determined to share in the danger, appeared on the field, with three regiments of General Learned's brigade, and made a spirited attack upon the center, composed of Hessian troops, which, at first was resisted with much vigor, but at the second charge, which was made with such irresistible force, Arnold, with a few brave followers dashing into the midst of them, that they broke and gave way in great disorder.

While the whole British line was thus broken and in much confusion, and the Americans pouring in their deadly fire on three sides of them, General Frazer, conspicuously mounted on an iron grey horse, was all activity, courage and vigilance, riding from one part of his division to another, and animating the troops by his example. Wherever he was present, everything prospered, and, when confusion appeared in any part of the line, order and energy were restored by his arrival. About this time Colonel Morgan, who with his rifle corps, was immediately opposed to Frazer's division, at the suggestion of Arnold, took a few of his riflemen aside, among whom was the celebrated marksman, Timothy Murphy; men in whose fidelity, and fatal precision of aim, he could repose the most perfect confidence, and said to them, "That gallant officer is General Frazer; I admire and respect him, *but it is necessary that he should die*—take your stations in that cluster of bushes and do your duty." Within a few moments, General Frazer fell, mortally wounded, and was carried off the field by a few grenadiers.

How far such personal designation is justifyable, has often been questioned, but those who vindicate war at all, contend, that to shoot a distinguished officer, and thus to accelerate the conclusion of a bloody battle, operates to save lives, and that it is, *morally,* no worse to kill an illustrious than an obscure individual; a *Frazer* than a common soldier; a *Lawrence* than a common sailor.

Soon after General Frazer fell, a reinforcement of three thousand New-York militia, under General Ten Broeck, came on the field, when the whole British line, commanded by Burgoyne in person, and in about fifty minutes after the action commenced, gave way and precipitately retreated within their entrenchments, hotly pursued by the victorious Americans, and leaving two twelve pounders and six six pounders on the field—with the loss of about two hundred officers and men killed and wounded, and as many prisoners, and among them the flower of his officers, viz: Brigadier-General Frazer; Major Ackland, commanding the grenadiers; Sir Francis Clark, his first aid-de-camp; Major Williams, commanding officer of the artillery; Captain Mooney, deputy quarter-master-general, and many others.

An interesting incident respecting Major Ackland I will here insert, while I leave the two armies to close the most important battle fought during the Revolutionary war; an account of which, shall immediately after be given.

While pursuing the flying enemy, passing over killed and wounded, Wilkinson says, he heard a voice exclaim,—"Protect me sir against that boy!" Turning his head, he saw a lad thirteen or fourteen years of age, deliberately aiming at a wounded officer, lying in the angle of a worm fence. The purpose of the boy was arrested—the officer proved to be the brave Major Ackland, who had commanded the grenadiers, and was wounded in both legs. He was immediately sent to head quarters. The story of Major Ackland has been rendered familiar to all, even before escaping the nursery, by the interesting narrative of Lady Harriet, his wife, who was with the army, and who, two days after the battle, came to the American camp, under a flag, to join her husband. The incident, from the embellishment it received, was touching and romantic. When divested of its poetry, however, and reduced to the plain matter of fact, according to the late General Dearborn, which he authorized to be published, the affair was not so very extraordinary that it might not have been enacted by any other pretty woman, under the same circumstances, who loved her husband. Major Ackland, who was conveyed from the field of battle, to my present kitchen, then General Poor's quarters, where his wounds were dressed, and where he remained several days on account of their excessive inflammation, was there visited by Lady Harriet, who remained with him, and was treated with all possible courtesy, until he was conveyed to Albany, when she was permitted to follow him. Major Ackland was a gallant officer and a generous foe. While in New-York, on parole, he did all in his power to favor the treatment of distinguished American prisoners. After his return to England, he sacrificed his life in defence of American honor. Having procured a regiment, at a dinner of military men, the courage of the Americans was questioned. He repelled the imputation with decision. High words ensued, in the course of which Ackland gave the lie direct to a subordinate officer named Lloyd. A meeting was the consequence, in which he was shot through the head. Lady Harriet lost her senses, and continued deranged two years, after which she married the Rev. Mr. Brudenell, the same gentleman who had accompanied her from the camp of Burgoyne, to that of General Gates, in search of her wounded husband.

CHAPTER VIII

But to resume. The British troops had scarcely entered their lines, when the Americans, led by Arnold, pressed forward, under a destructive fire of grape shot and musketry, assaulted their works throughout their whole extent, from right to left, and a long, arduous and bloody conflict ensued, in which many brave men fell on both sides.

This long and bloody contest was now carried on between the British behind their works, and the Americans entirely exposed, or partially sheltered by trees, stumps or hollows at various distances; and the tremendous roar of artillery, from one extremity of the line to the other, filling the air with one continual volume of smoke and blaze—the constant peal of small arms, hurling, in rapid succession, their leaden messengers of death —and bomb after bomb, with their fiery trails, flaming, like meteors, through the thick and darkened atmosphere, presented a scene "awfully sublime," and beyond the power of description:

And such as have ne'er seen them, most surely would
    fear,
The stars had dissolved, and the last judgment was
    near!

In the midst of this dreadful scene of blood and carnage, Arnold, at the head of a band of brave fellows, from Poor's and Patterson's brigades, rushing, like tigers, into the camp of Lord Balcarras, and encountering the British troops at the point of the bayonet, dealt death and destruction in every quarter. From thence, spurred boldly on, he dashed through thick and thin, to the extreme right of the British camp, occupied by the Hessian troops, where he was still more successful.

This right flank defence of the enemy, occupied by the German corps under Colonel Breyman, consisted in a great measure, of a breast work of rails piled horizontally between perpendicular pickets, driven into the earth, *en potence* to the rest of his line, and extended about two hundred yards across an open field, and was covered on the high ground on the right, by a battery of two guns. The interval from the left of this defence to the light infantry, under Lord Balcarras, was committed to the defence of the Provincialists, who occupied a log house and barn, then owned by Thomas Leggett. The Germans were encamped immediately behind the rail breastwork, and the ground in front of it declined in a very gentle slope, for about one hundred and twenty yards, when it sunk abruptly. The American troops had formed a line under this declivity, and covered breast high, were warmly engaged with the Germans. From this position, about sunset, Brigadier-General Learned advanced towards the enemy with his brigade in open column, with Colonel Jackson's regiment, then in command of Lieut.-Colonel Brooks, in front. On his approach, he inquired where he could *"put in"* with most advantage. A slack fire was observed at an opening between the left of the Germans, and light infantry, occupied by the Provincialists; and the general was recommended to incline to the right and attack that point. He did so with great gallantry; the Provincialists abandoned their position and fled. The German flank, by this means being left uncovered, and Arnold arriving at the moment, and taking the lead of Learned's brigade, they were vigorously assaulted, overturned in a few minutes, and retreated in great disorder—leaving their gallant commander mortally wounded, on the field, and all their tents, artillery, and baggage in possession of the victors.

By dislodging this corps, the whole British encampment was laid open to the Americans; but the extreme darkness of the night, the fatigue of the men, and disorder incident to undisciplined troops, after so desultory an action, put it out of the power of the Americans to improve the advantages.

This brilliant manœuvre with which the engagement was closed, the assault of the enemy's works and driving the Hessians from their encampment, was undoubtedly owing to the intrepidity of Arnold. He gave the order, and by his personal bravery set an example to the troops, which inspired them with ardor and hurried them onward. He was shot through the leg whilst riding gallantly into the sally-port, and his horse fell dead under him. The success of the assault was complete and crowned the day with victory.

Thus ended this battle, with most dreadful slaughter,
The pride and renown of the town of Stillwater;
A glorious one too, for on *it* hung the key,
That unlocked the tyrant's door, and set us all free!
'Twas the *bright* rising sun of our national morn—
The herald of "glad-tidings" to millions unborn!

At the commencement of the foregoing battle, Quarter-Master-General, Major Lewis, was directed to take eight men with him to the field, as messengers, to convey to General Gates, who remained at camp issuing his orders as circumstances required, such information, as might from time to time, be communicated to them, respecting the progress of the action, and whether for or against the Americans. At the same time the baggage of the army was all loaded up, and the cavalcade of teams, extended from a little south of the fort on the Heights, along the road for near half a mile, under the direction of Major Chandenette, as wagon-master, and to move according to orders from the commanding general. The first information that arrived, represented the British troops on the field to exceed the Americans, by so much, that it was thought the Americans would be forced to retire; when the teams were ordered to, "move on!" but by the time they could all be got under motion more favorable news arrived, when the orders were immediately countermanded, and the stentorian voice of the wagon-master was heard in the distance, "Halt!" Thus they continued alternately to move on and halt, until the joyful news "The British have retreated!" rang through the camp, and reached the attentive ears of the teamsters; and the scene that was then enacted, exhibited in its true spirit, the fire of patriotism that was kindled in the breast of every true American. No sooner had the exhilarating news reach these men, though in subordinate station, than they all with one accord, off with their hats—swung them around their heads, and gave three long, loud, and deafening cheers, Huzzah! Huzzah!! Huzzah!!! which, being wafted, as on the wings of the wind, was transmitted with such rapidity from one to another, that, by the time the victorious troops retired from the field of battle and returned to quarters, much elated with their success, the American camp was thronged with inhabitants from the surrounding country, and presented a scene of complicated horror and exultation. In one part, the harmonious sound of drums, the exhilarating tone of fifes, here and there, groups of soldiers shouting victory! victory! and all eager for another contest, gave animation and spirit to the scene; while in another, the hailing of sentinels, the rapidly moving of lights, the piercing cries of the wounded, and the doleful groans of the dying, proclaimed in language too plain to be misunderstood, the complicated horrors of war!

Accompanying the American army were a great number of women, principally foreigners, many of whom had husbands or brothers in the action, and many who followed merely for the sake of plunder, as was manifested during the night after the action of the 7th October. The next morning after the battle, every man that was left dead on the field, and even those who were supposed to be mortally wounded, and not yet dead, but helpless, were found stript of their clothing, which rendered it almost impossible to distinguish between American and British. But *during* the action, a heart-rending, and yet to some a laughable, scene took place in the American camp, and probably the same in the British. In the heat of the battle, and while the cannon were constantly roaring like oft peals of distant thunder, and making the earth to quake from its very foundation, some of those women, wringing their hands, apparently in the utmost distress, and frantically tearing their hair in the agony of their feelings, were heard to cry out, in the most lamentable exclamations, "Och, my husband! my poor husband! Lord Jesus, spare my poor husband!" which would be often repeated, and sometimes by fifteen or twenty voices at once; while the more hardened ones, and those rejoicing in the prospect of plunder, would break out in blasphemous imprecations, exclaiming, "D—n your poor husband, you can get another!" And in this manner the scene continued during the action; and I have heard it observed by those who were present, that they could not help smiling, even through their tears, at the pitiful exhibition.

The British loss during this day was about

seven hundred killed,* wounded and prisoners, and Burgoyne himself very narrowly escaped, one ball having passed through his hat, and his waistcoat was torn by another.

The American loss was inconsiderable, and did not exceed one hundred and fifty killed* and wounded. General Arnold was among the latter; who, though he had not been reinstated in his command since the dispute with General Gates, before mentioned, rode about the field, giving orders in every direction,

---

* The British and Hessian troops who were killed in the foregoing actions, were slightly covered with earth and brush on the battle fields, apparently unlamented by friend or foe. It was not an uncommon thing, after the land was cleared and began to be cultivated, to see five, ten, and in some instances, even twenty human skulls piled up on different stumps about the fields; and I have myself when a boy seen human bones thickly strewed about on the ground, which had been turned out with the plough.

* A little west and south of the fort on the Heights, now lie mouldering into dust, the remains of many of those martyrs to the cause of freedom, who fell in the battles of the 19th Sept. and 7th Oct., and not a stone, or other memento, to mark the hallowed spot. Often, when I am passing over the soil "fattened" by their blood, I can almost imagine to myself I hear a voice crying from the ground, O, my country! my beloved country! how long shall we thy fallen sons be thus neglected? And the very hills seem to rëecho back the mournful sound, how long! how long!

sometimes in direct opposition to those of the commander, at others leading a platoon in person, and exposing himself to the hottest fire of the enemy. Being the highest officer in rank that appeared on the field, his orders were obeyed when practicable; but all accounts agree that his conduct was rash in the extreme, indicating rather the frenzy of a mad man, than the considerate wisdom of an experienced general. He threw himself heedlessly into the most exposed situations, brandishing his sword in the air, animating his troops, and urging them forward.

It is a curious fact, that an officer who had really no command in the army, was the leader in one of the most spirited and important battles of the Revolution. His madness, or rashness, or whatever it may be called, resulted most fortunately for himself. The wound he received at the moment of rushing into the very arms of danger and death, added fresh lustre to his military glory, and was a new claim to public favor and applause. Wilkinson ascribed his wild temerity to *intoxication,* but Major Armstrong, who assisted in removing him from the field, was satisfied that this was not true. Others said he took opium. This is conjecture, unsustained by proofs of any kind, and consequently improbable. His vagaries may perhaps be sufficiently explained by the extraordinary circumstances of wounded pride, anger and desperation, in which he was placed. Congress relented, though with an ill grace at so late a period, and authorized Gen. Washington to send him a commission, giving him the full rank he had claimed.

General Gates remained in camp during the whole action, that he might be the better enabled to order and regulate the various movements, as circumstances should require.

The night of the seventh of October, was a most critical one for the royal army; in the course of it, they abandoned their camp and moved to the high ground, contiguous to the river, and immediately in rear of their hospital. On the morning of the eighth, the American army moved forward and took possession of the abandoned camp, from which they kept up a random fire of artillery and small arms during the whole day. Burgoyne's troops were all day under arms in expectation of another attack, and indicating by their movements that they intended a still further retreat. In the occasional skirmishes of the day, General Lincoln was shot in the leg, while riding near the line, by some of the enemy's marksmen from the opposite side of the ravine.

The gallant Frazer, who had been mortally wounded the day before, died at eight o'clock on the morning of the eighth. On the evening of his fall, when it was rendered certain that he could not recover, he sent for General Burgoyne, and requested that he might be buried at six o'clock the following evening in the great redoubt, on the hill. It was a subject of complaint against Burgoyne, that in order to comply with his request, he delayed his retreat, and thus contributed to the misfortunes of his army. Be that as it may, the dying soldier's request was observed to the letter. At the hour appointed, the body was borne to the hill that had been indicated, attended by the generals and their retinues; the funeral service was read by the chaplain, Mr. Brudenell, and the corpse interred while the balls of the American cannon were flying around and above the assembled mourners.

The Baroness Reidesell, who with several other ladies of distinction, accompanied the army of Burgoyne, states, that General Gates protested afterwards that had he known what was going on, he would have stopped the fire immediately. And General Winslow, who commanded the gun which was fired on this occasion, says, that as soon as they discovered that it was a funeral procession, they ceased firing shot, and commenced firing minute-guns—a high minded mark of respect, sometimes shown, when a distinguished enemy is buried.

This must have been a solemn spectacle, and General Burgoyne himself describes it with his usual eloquence and felicity of expression:—"The incessant cannonade during the solemnity; the steady attitude and unaltered voice with which the chaplain officiated, though frequently covered with dust, which the shot threw up on all sides of him; the mute but expressive mixture of sensibility and indignation upon every countenance; these objects will remain to the last of life upon the mind of every man who was present. The growing duskiness added to the scenery, and the whole marked a character of that juncture, that would make one of the finest subjects for the pencil of a master, that the field ever exhibited. To the canvass, and to the faithful page of a more important historian, gallant friend! I consign thy memory. There may thy talents, thy manly virtues, their progress and their period, find due distinction; and long may they survive, after the frail record of my pen shall be forgotten.''

The soldier who shot General Frazer, was Timothy Murphy, a Virginian, and belonged to Morgan's rifle corps, in which he distinguished himself as a marksman, and excited much interest while in camp. After the capture of Burgoyne, the company to which he belonged was ordered to Schoharie, where it remained until their term of service expired. When the company was disbanded, Murphy and some others remained, and served in the militia; his skill in the desultory war which the Indians carry on, gave him so high a reputation, that though not nominally the commander, he usually directed all the movements of the scouts that were sent out, and on many important occasions the commanding officers found it dangerous to neglect his advice; his *double rifle,* his skill as a marksman, and his fleetness either in retreat or pursuit, made him an object both of dread and of vengeance to the Indians: they formed many plans to destroy him, but he always eluded them, and sometimes made them suffer for their temerity.

He fought the Indians with their own weapons. When circumstances permitted, he tomahawked and scalped his fallen enemy; he boasted after the war that he had slain forty of the enemy with his own hand, more than half of whom he had scalped; he took delight in perilous adventures, and seemed to love danger for danger's sake. Tradition has preserved the account of many of his exploits; but there are so many versions of the same story, and so much evident fiction mixed with the truth, that the author will give but a single instance as proof of the dread with which he was regarded by the Indians.

They were unable to conjecture how he could discharge his rifle twice without having time to reload; and his singular good fortune in escaping unhurt, led them to suppose that he was attended by some invisible being, who warded off *their* bullets, and sped *his* with unerring certainty to the mark. When they had learned the mystery of his double-barrelled rifle, they were careful not to expose themselves too much until he had fired twice, knowing that he must have time to reload his piece before he could do them further injury.

One day having separated from his party, he was pursued by a number of Indians, all of whom he outran excepting one; Murphy turned round, fired upon this Indian, and killed him. Supposing that the others had given up the pursuit he stopped to strip the dead, when the rest of his pursuers came in sight. He snatched the rifle of his fallen foe, and with it killed one of his pursuers; the rest, now sure of their prey, with a yell of joy heedlessly rushed on, hoping to make him their prisoner; he was ready to drop down with fatigue, and was likely to be overtaken, when turning round, he discharged the remaining barrel of his rifle, and killed the foremost of the Indians; the rest astonished at his firing three times in succession, fled, crying out that he could shoot all day without loading.

In stature, Murphy was about five feet six inches, and very well proportioned, with dark complexion, and an eye that would kindle and flash like the very lightning when excited. He was exceedingly quick in all his motions, and possessed an iron frame that nothing apparently could affect: And what is very remarkable, his body was never wounded or scarred during the whole war.

It was evident from the movements in Burgoyne's camp, on the evening of the eighth, that he was preparing to retreat; but the American troops having, in the delirium of joy consequent upon their victory, neglected to draw and eat their rations—being withal not a little fatigued with the two days exertions, fell back to their camp, which had been left standing in the morning. Retreat was indeed the only alternative remaining to the British commander, since it was now quite certain that he could not cut his way through the American army, and his supplies were reduced to a short allowance for five days. That commander, who, in the commencement of the campaign, had uttered in his general orders the memorable sentiment, "this army must not retreat," was now compelled to seek his safety by stealing away in the night from his victorious enemy, and leaving his hospital, containing more than four hundred sick and wounded, to the mercy of General Gates, who in this as in all other instances, exhibited towards the enemy the greatest humanity and kindness. Numerous fires were lighted—several tents left standing, and the retreat was ordered to be conducted with the greatest secrecy. The army commenced its retrograde motion at nine o'clock on the evening of the 8th of October, pursuing the river road along the flats. It moved all night, and made a halt in the morning at Do-ve-gat, (Coveville,) where it remained during the principal part of the ninth, it being an excessively rainy day.

While the British army were halted here, a detachment of about three hundred American troops, who had been sent on to harass them in their retreat, overtook and made an attack upon their rear guard, under General Phillips, about a mile below, but the heavy rain prevented their effecting much.

Before the British troops commenced their retrograde march, the Baroness Reidesel suggested to Lady Ackland, the propriety of rejoining her husband, to whom she might be of great service in his present situation, and again at this place strongly impressed upon her its importance. Yielding to her constant and friendly advice, Lady Harriet sent a message to General Burgoyne, through his aid-de-camp, Lord Petersham, to beg his permission to leave the army. It has been represented that the British commander was thunderstruck at the application, but gave her leave to proceed, although he was utterly unable to afford any assistance.

After her fatigue, and after being drenched in a heavy rain of twelve hours, she instantly proceeded on. The celebrated letter of General Burgoyne to General Gates on the occasion, has often been admired, and which is here inserted as a specimen of that talent for composition, which afterwards distinguished the author of the "Narrative," and several elegant comedies, well known to the reading public.

"Sir—Lady Harriet Ackland, a lady of the first distinction of family, rank and personal virtues, is under such concern on account of Major Ackland, her husband, wounded, and a prisoner in your hands, that I cannot refuse her request to commit her to your protection. What ever general impropriety there may be in persons in my situation and yours to solicit favors, I cannot see the uncommon perseverance in every female grace and exaltation of character of this lady, and her very hard fortune, without testifying that your attentions to her will lay me under obligations.

I am, sir, your ob't serv't,
J. BURGOYNE."

From the wife of a soldier she obtained a little spirits and water, and with this to sustain her, she set out in an open boat, and sailed down the river, during a violent storm of rain and wind, accompanied by the British chaplain, Brudenell, her own waiting maid, Sarah Pollard, and her husband's valet de chambre, who had been severely wounded in searching through the field of battle for his master, when first missing.

An impression has gone abroad, sanctioned not only by gentlemen belonging to Burgoyne's army, but by that general himself, that this ill-fated and amiable female was kept all night in the boat, and not permitted to land until morning. This is not the fact. In ten minutes after the boat was hailed by the sentinel of the advance guard, she was invited to the quarters of Major Dearborn, (since so distinguished as a general officer,) where she received every attention in his power to bestow, and was made happy by the intelligence of her husband's safety. In the morning before sunrise, through the politeness of General Gates, she was conveyed to the quarters of General Poor on the Heights, to her wounded husband; where she remained until he was conveyed to Albany. The resolution and firmness of this lady excited a great sensation throughout the American camp, while the tender devotion which she displayed towards her husband, "won her golden opinions" of all sorts of people.

While the British army on their advance were encamped at Do-ve-gat, (Coveville) Major Ackland's tent took fire, and Lady Harriet and himself were nearly lost in the flames. The Major being with the advance guard, and obliged to be very diligent in attending to his command, in consequence of the difficulty and danger of his position, kept a candle burning in his tent. A Newfoundland dog, of which they were very fond, unfortunately pushed the candle from a table or chair where it was standing; it fell against the side of the tent, and instantly the whole was in a blaze. A soldier who was keeping guard near them, rushed in and dragged Major Ackland from the flames, while Lady Harriet crept out almost unconsciously through the back part of the tent. When she looked round she saw with horror her husband rushing into the flames in search of her. Again the soldier brought him out, though not without considerable injury to both. Everything in the tent was consumed; but the Major and his lady were too happy to see each other in safety to regret the loss of their camp equipage.

It may not be amiss to state, that this admired and beautiful woman had already been subjected to great inconveniences and distress, before the army arrived at Saratoga. She had been distinguished by her devotion and unremitting attention to her husband, when he lay sick at Chamblee, in a miserable hut, encountering every inconvenience, and subjected to every privation. She was indeed not only the idol of her husband, but the admiration of the army, continually making little presents to the officers belonging to her husband's corps, whenever she had anything among her stores worthy of acceptance. She experienced in return from them every attention which could mitigate the hardships she daily was obliged to encounter.

When her husband was wounded at Hubbardton, she again, like a guardian angel, hovered round him, and watched him until he was restored to health. The moment she heard of his being wounded she hastened from Montreal, where she had intended to remain, and crossed the lake in opposition to her husband's injunctions, resolved to share his fate and be separated from him no more.

CHAPTER IX

Previous to the action of the seventh, General Gates, anticipating the retreat of the enemy, had ordered General Fellows, with about fifteen hundred men, as before mentioned, to cross the river, and take post on the heights opposite the Saratoga ford, supposing that he might be able to reinforce him before Burgoyne could reach that place. But the retreat of the British army being earlier than he expected, and the circumstances of the heavy rain on the ninth, preventing him from pursuing immediately with the main army, or sending off any considerable detachment, General Fellows was placed in a critical situation, and nothing saved his detachment from destruction or capture, but the very slow movements of Burgoyne, occasioned by the heavy rain and the badness of the roads; so that he did not reach Saratoga (Schuylerville,) until the morning of the tenth. By this time General Fellows had received orders to recross the river and endeavor to oppose their passage, which he did just as the front of the British army crossed

Fish creek, and in time to post himself advantageously on the opposite side of the river. On the evening before, his camp was so entirely unguarded, that Lieutentant-Colonel Southerland, who had been sent forward by Burgoyne to reconnoitre, marched round it without meeting a sentinel, and was so strongly impressed with the conviction that he could surprise him, that he solicited permission to attack him with his single regiment, and it was perhaps fortunate for General Fellows that Burgoyne refused. In the mean time several other bodies of militia were posted, to intercept the retreat of Burgoyne, in various directions, and one detachment was ordered to march immediately to Fort Edward, and take possession before any part of Burgoyne's troops could reach it. The rain on the ninth and morning of the tenth, prevented General Gates from marching until about noon. When the advance of the army reached Saratoga, about four o'clock in the afternoon, the British were encamped on the heights beyond Fish creek; their boats lay at the mouth of the creek and a fatigue party were at work in removing the baggage from the creek to the heights. Gen. Fellows with his corps were on the opposite bank of the river, with a couple of small field pieces on the flats, playing upon the enemy's fatigue party. General Gates on his arrival posted the army in several lines on the heights about a mile in the rear of Fish creek, with Colonel Morgan's corps in front. Under the idea that the enemy would retreat in the night, General Gates gave orders that the army should advance at *reveillee* in the morning of the eleventh. A small detachment had been sent off by Burgoyne to possess themselves of Fort Edward, but Col. Cochran with about two hundred men, had already taken possession of that place, and on the arrival of the British detachment at Deadman's point, on the opposite side of the river, piles of logs and brush, which had been collected, on the first rise of Fort Edward hill, by the British on their advance, having now become dry, were set on fire in the night, which at a distance, had the appearance of a large encampment. When the British troops saw the fire they, supposing the American forces to be as numerous in front as in their rear, hastily retreated to their camp at Fish creek.

The movement of this detachment had given rise to the information which deceived General Gates, that the whole British army had moved off, leaving a small guard only in the camp to take care of the baggage and stores. Upon this intelligence it was determined to attack the camp early in the morning; and Brigadier-Generals Nixon and Glover were ordered to cross the creek with their brigades for this purpose.

Colonel Morgan advancing with his corps at daylight agreeably to orders fell in with the enemy's picket, by whom he was fired upon, and lost a lieutenant and several privates. This induced him to believe that the enemy had not moved as supposed, in which case his situation would be extremely critical, as the fog was so thick that nothing could be seen at the distance of twenty yards; a winding creek was in his rear, and he was unacquainted with the grounds. In this dilemma he was met by the deputy-adjutant-general, Colonel Wilkinson, who had been sent out by General Gates, for the purpose of reconnoitering. Wilkinson returned immediately to communicate this intelligence to the General, and Patterson's and Learned's brigades, both under the command of the latter, and Colonel Woodbridge's regiment, were sent to the support of Morgan.

In the meantime the whole army advanced as far as the ridge between the church and Fish creek, where they halted. Generals Nixon and Glover were in advance, marching according to orders to the attack of the camp. Nixon had already crossed the creek, and surprised a British picket in old Fort Hardy, and Glover was preparing to follow him, when a deserter from the enemy was observed fording the creek, from whom information was received that Burgoyne with his whole army were still in his camp. This was confirmed by the capture of a reconnoitering party of a subaltern and thirty-five men, by the advance guard of fifty under Captain Goodale, of Putnam's regiment, who discovered them through the fog just as he reached the bank of the creek, and making a resolute charge upon them, took them without firing a gun. General Gates was at this time a mile in the rear, and before this intelligence could be communicated to him, and orders received for the two brigadiers to desist and recross the creek, the fog cleared up, and exposed to view the whole British army under arms.

A heavy fire of artillery and small arms was immediately opened upon Nixon's brigade, which was in advance, and they retreated in considerable disorder across the creek, with a trifling loss, and resumed their position.

General Learned had in the meantime reached Morgan's corps with his two brigades, and was advancing rapidly to the attack, in obedience to a standing order which had been issued the day before, "That in case of an attack against any point, whether front, flank or rear, the troops are to fall on the enemy at all quarters." He had arrived within two hundred yards of Burgoyne's strongest post, and in a few minutes more would have been engaged under great disadvantage, when Colonel Wilkinson reached him with intelligence that our right wing had given way, and that it would be prudent for him to retreat. Being without authority from General Gates to order it, the brave old general hesitated to obey, in opposition to the standing order, until Lieutenant-Colonels Brooks and Tupper and some other officers coming up, a sort of council was held, and the proposition to retreat was approved.

The moment they turned their backs, the enemy who had been calmly expecting their advance, opened a fire upon them, which continued until they were masked by the woods.

General Gates was immediately informed of the incident; he revoked all the orders he had given, and directed that the troops should be reconducted to their several positions; Morgan at the same time taking post in flank and rear of the British right.

The following facts respecting Col. Cochran, I obtained through the politeness of Miss Caroline Ogden, an interesting maiden lady, and grand-daughter of the colonel, who now resides with J. T. M'Cown, Esq., in the city of Troy.

Colonel Cochran having been sent to Canada as a spy, his mission was suspected, and a large bounty offered for his head. While there he was taken sick, and knowing that he was suspected, concealed himself, for the space of a few days, in a brush heap, within about two miles of the American lines, unable to make his escape, or even to walk. Having suffered much from his sickness and want of nourishment, and having discovered a log cabin at considerable distance from where he was concealed, and the only one in sight, he crept to it on his hands and knees, for the purpose of soliciting assistance. On his approach to the rear of the cabin, he heard three men in earnest conversation, and as it happened he was the

subject of their discourse. Having heard of
the heavy bounty that was offered for the
Colonel, and having seen a man in the vicinity
a few days before, answering the description
of him, they were then forming their plans,
and expressing their determination to find his
whereabouts, and take him for the sake of
the bounty. One of the men was the owner
of the cabin, whose wife was also present,
and the others were his brother and brother-
in-law. Soon after this conversation took
place, and the three men having departed in
pursuit, he crept into the cabin, and frankly
told the woman, who seemed favorably impressed towards him, on account of his almost
helpless condition, that he had overheard the
conversation, and that *he* was the man of whom
they were in search, and that he should throw
himself entirely upon her mercy, and trust to
her fidelity for protection, which she very
kindly promised him, to the utmost of her
ability. Having administered some restora-
tives, which seemed to give relief, and given
him some suitable nourishment, he lay down
on a bed in the room, for the purpose of taking some repose, which he very much needed.
After the men had been absent some three

hours, they again returned, when she concealed him in a closet, or sort of cupboard, standing by the side of the fire-place, and shut the door, taking good care while the men were in the house, to keep near it herself, that if anything should be wanted from within, she might be ready to get it herself. During the time the men were in the cabin, they expressed much confidence in the belief, that the colonel was concealed somewhere in the vicinity, and named many places in which they intended to search for him; all of which he in his place of concealment overheard. Having taken some food, and otherwise prepared themselves, the men again departed, in order to renew their search.

Soon after they retired, and the woman considering the Colonel's present situation not long safe, she proposed that he should conceal himself at some distance from the cabin, where she might clandestinely bring him food, and render him such other assistance as he needed, and accordingly directed him to take post on a certain hill about half a mile off, where he might be able to discover any person on their approach, and to flee, if he was able, and it became necessary. On his manifesting an inclination to resume his former position in the brush heap, which was in the midst of quite a patch of ground that had been cut over for a fallow, she told him that her husband intended to burn it over the next day, and in that case he would certainly be discovered, or perish in the conflagration; upon which he submitted entirely to her proposition and directions, and crept along to the hill in the best way he could. He remained sometime in this place of concealment, undiscovered by any one except this faithful Rahab of the forest, who rendered him suitable and timely assistance, and like a good Samaritan poured in the "oil and the wine," until his strength was in a measure restored, and he was again enabled to return to his country and his home.

Some years after the close of the war, and while the Colonel lived at Ticonderoga, he accidently came across this kind hearted woman, whose name, I much regret, I have not been able to ascertain, and rewarded her handsomely for her fidelity.

Colonel Cochran died 1822, near Sandy Hill, Washington county, New York, much lamented by a large circle of friends and acquaintances, and was buried in the family burying ground at Fort Edward.

Here too, those warrior sires with honor rest,
Who braved in freedom's cause the valiant breast;
Lo! here they rest, who every danger braved,
Unmarked, untrophied, 'mid the soil they saved.

A few days more of anxiety, fatigue and suffering remained for the British army. They had lost part of their provision batteaux, taken by the Americans while on their retreat, and the rest being exposed to imminent danger, the small stock of provisions remaining, was landed under a heavy fire, and hauled up the heights. On these heights near to the flats bordering on the river, was formed their fortified camp, extending over half a mile in rear, and strengthened by artillery; most of their artillery however, was back on the plain, and on an elevated piece of ground northeast of the present village of Schuylerville. Gen. Gates's army was encamped on the south side of Fish creek and parallel to it, the corps of Colonel Morgan lay west and northwest of the British army, and General Fellows, whose forces were now increased to two thousand men, was on the east side of the Hudson, ready to dispute the passage of that stream should it be attempted. Fort Edward was occupied by the Americans—a fortified camp was formed on the high ground between this fort and Fort George, and numerous parties were stationed up and down the river; thus the desperate resolution which had been taken in General Burgoyne's camp, of abandoning their artillery and baggage and (with no more provisions than they could carry on their backs,) forcing their way by a rapid night march, in this manner gaining one of the lakes, was rendered abortive.

Every part of the royal army was now exposed, not only to cannon balls, but to rifle shot; not a single place of safety could be found, not a corner where a council could be held, a dinner taken in peace, or where the sick and the wounded, the females and the children could find an asylum. Even the access to the river was rendered very hazardous by the numerous rifle shot, and the army was soon distressed for want of water. General Reidesel, and his lady and children, were often obliged to drink wine instead of water, and they had no way to procure the latter, except that a soldier's wife ventured to the river for them, and the Americans, out of respect to her sex, did not fire at her.

To protect his family from shot, the Baron de Reidesel, soon after their arrival at Saratoga, directed them to take shelter in Lemson's house (now Mrs. Bushee's,) about a mile up the river, and opposite to the mouth of Batten kill. They had scarcely reached it, before a terrible cannonade from the heights on the opposite side of the river was directed against that very house, upon the mistaken idea, that all the generals were assembled in it; "Alas," adds the Baroness, "it contained none but wounded and women; we were at last obliged to resort to the cellar for refuge, and in one corner of this I remained the whole day, my children sleeping on the earth with their heads in my lap, and in the same situation, I passed a sleepless night. Eleven cannon balls passed through the house, and we could distinctly hear them roll away. One poor soldier who was lying on a table, for the purpose of having his leg amputated, was struck by a shot which carried away the other; his comrades had left him, and when we found him he was in the corner of the room, into which he had crept, more dead than alive, scarcely breathing. My reflections on the danger to which my husband was exposed, now agonized me exceedingly, and the thoughts of my children, and the necessity of struggling for their preservation, alone sustained me. In this horrid situation we remained six days." In such a state of circumstances, it was alike impossible to advance or remain as they were; and the longer they delayed to take a definitive resolution, the more desperate became their situation. Burgoyne, therefore, immediately called a council of war, at which not only the generals and field officers, but all the captains of companies were invited to assist. While they deliberated, the balls of the Americans whistled around them, and frequently pierced even the tent where the council was convened. It was determined unanimously to open a treaty and enter into a convention with General Gates.

On the 14th of October, General Burgoyne sent Major Kingston to the head quarters of General Gates, with a proposition for "a cessation of arms, during the time necessary to communicate the preliminary terms; by which in any extremity he and the army mean to abide." General Gates had already prepared a schedule of the terms upon which he was willing to treat. This schedule evinced that he was well acquainted with the distresses of the British, and was drawn up in terms of extreme liberality. To the 9th article of General Burgoyne's proposition, General Gates affixed the following answer:

The *capitulation* to be finished by two o'clock *this day*, the 15th, and the troops march from their encampment at five, and be in readiness to move towards Boston to-morrow morning. These preliminary articles and their answers, being sent to General Burgoyne, produced the immediate return of his messenger with the following note. "The eight first preliminary articles of Lieutenant General Burgoyne's proposals, and the 2d, 3d, and 4th of those of Major-General Gates, of yesterday, being agreed to, the formation of the proposed treaty is out of dispute: but the several subordinate articles and regulations necessarily springing from these preliminaries, and requiring explanation and precision, between the parties, before a definitive treaty can be safely executed, a longer time than that mentioned by General Gates in his answer to the ninth article, becomes indispensably necessary. Lieutenant-General Burgoyne is willing to appoint two officers immediately, to meet two others from Major-General Gates, to propound, discuss, and settle those subordinate articles, in order that the treaty in due form may be executed as soon as possible.''

This meeting took place on the afternoon of the 15th, and the parties mutually signed articles of capitulation, or *convention,* as General Burgoyne wished to have it designated. A copy of the convention was to be signed by General Burgoyne, and delivered the next morning.

In the night, an express arrived at the British camp from General Clinton, with the intelligence that he had moved up the Hudson, reduced Fort Montgomery, and penetrated as far as Esopus. This information seemed to revive a hope of safety in the breast of Burgoyne; he therefore called a meeting of the officers to declare, whether in a case of extremity, the soldiers were in a situation to fight, and whether they considered the public faith as pledged by the verbal convention. A great number answered, that the soldiers, debilitated by fatigue and hunger, were unable to make resistance; all were decidedly of the opinion, that the public faith was engaged.

Burgoyne alone manifested a contrary opinion. Meanwhile General Gates, apprised of these hesitations of the British commander, and the new hopes which occasioned them, formed his troops in order of battle on the morning of the sixteenth, and sent to inform Burgoyne, that the stipulated time being arrived, he must either sign the articles, or prepare himself for battle. The Englishman no longer hesitated, but took his resolution; he signed the paper, which was in the following words:

Articles of Convention between Lieutenant-General Burgoyne and Major-General Gates.

1st. "The troops under Lieutenant-General Burgoyne, to march out of their camp with the honors of war, and the artillery of entrenchments, to the verge of the river where the old fort stood, where the arms and artillery are to be left; the arms to be piled by word of command from their own officers.

2d. A free passage to be granted to the army under Lieutenant-General Burgoyne to Great Britain, on condition of not serving again in North America during the present contest; and the port of Boston is assigned for the entry of transports to receive the troops, whenever General Howe shall so order.

3d. Should any cartel take place, by which the army under General Burgoyne, or any part of it, may be exchanged, the foregoing articles to be void as far as such exchange should be made.

4th. The army under Lieutenant-General Burgoyne, to march to Massachusetts Bay, by the easiest, most expeditious, and convenient route, and be quartered in, near, or as convenient as possible to Boston, that the march of the troops may not be delayed, when the transports shall arrive to receive them.

5th. The troops to be supplied on their march, and during their being in quarters, with provisions by Gen. Gates's orders, at the same rate of rations as the troops of his own army; and if possible, the officers' horses and cattle are to be supplied with forage at the usual rates.

6th. All officers to retain their carriages, battle-horses, and other cattle, and no baggage to be molested or searched; Lieutenant-General Burgoyne giving his honor that there are no public stores secreted therein. Major-General Gates will of course take the necessary measures for the due performance of this article. Should any carriages be wanted during the march for the transportation of officers' baggage, they are if possible, to be supplied.

7th. Upon the march, and during the time the army shall remain in quarters in Massachusetts Bay, the officers are not as far as circumstances will admit, to be separated from their men. The officers are to be quartered according to rank, and are not to be hindered from assembling their men for roll-call, and the necessary purposes of regularity.

8th. All corps whatever of General Burgoyne's army whether composed of sailors, batteaux men, artificers, drivers, independent companies, and follow-artificers, drivers, independent companies, and followers of the army of whatever country, shall be included in every respect as British subjects.

9th. All Canadians, and persons belonging to the Canadian establishment, consisting of sailors, batteaux men, artificers, drivers, independent companies, and many other followers of the army, who come under no particular description, are to be permitted to return there; they are to be conducted immediately by the shortest route to the first British post on Lake George, are to be supplied with provisions in the same manner as the other troops, are to be bound by the same condition of not serving during the present contest in North America.

10th. Passports to be immediately granted for three officers not exceeding the rank of captains, who shall be appointed by Lieutenant-General Burgoyne, to carry despatches to Sir William Howe, Sir Guy Carleton, and to Great Britain by the way of New York; and Maj. General Gates engages the public faith, that these despatches shall not be opened. These officers are to set out immdiately after receiving their despatches, and are to travel the shortest route, and in the most expeditious manner.

11th. During the stay of the troops in Massachusetts Bay, the officers are to be admitted on parole, and are to be allowed to wear their side arms.

12th. Should the army under Lieutenant-General Burgoyne find it necessary to send for their clothing and other baggage to Canada, they are to be permitted to do it in the most convenient manner, and the necessary passports granted for that purpose.

13th. These articles are to be mutually signed and exchanged to-morrow morning, at nine o'clock, and the troops under Lieutenant-General Burgoyne, are to march out of their entrenchments at three o'clock in the afternoon.

(Signed)   HORATIO GATES, *Maj. Gen.*
(Signed)   J. BURGOYNE, *Lieut. Gen.*
Saratoga, Oct. 16, 1777.

To prevent any doubts that might arise from Lieutenant-General Burgoyne's name not being mentioned in the above treaty, Major-General Gates hereby declares, that he is understood to be comprehended in it, as fully as if his name had been specifically mentioned.

                      HORATIO GATES.

The brass artillery captured from Burgoyne at various times during the campaign, amounted to forty-two pieces, constituting one of the most elegant trains ever brought into the field; five thousand stand of arms; six thousand dozen of cartridges; and a number of ammunition wagons, travelling forges, shot, carcases, shells, &c., &c., also fell into the hands of the Americans. The whole number of troops surrendered by the convention amounted to five thousand, seven hundred and ninety-two, which, added to the number killed, wounded and captured in the several actions previous to the 17th of October, amounting to near five thousand, makes Burgoyne's total loss upwards of *ten thousand men.*

In the morning of the 17th, Colonel Wilkinson was directed to visit General Burgoyne in his camp, and accompany him to the green in front of old Fort Hardy, on the north bank of Fish creek, and near its intersection with the Hudson, where his army was to lay down their arms, from thence they rode to the margin of the river, which he surveyed with attention, and asked whether it was not fordable. "Certainly, sir; but do you observe the people on the opposite shore?" "Yes," he replied, "I have seen them too long!" He then proposed to be introduced to General Gates, and they crossed Fish creek, and proceeded to head-quarters, General Burgoyne in front, with his Adjutant-General Kingston, and his aids-de-camp Captain Lord Petersham, and Lieutenant Wilford behind him; then followed Major-General Phillips, the Baron Reidesel, and the other general officers, and their suits, according to rank. General Gates, advised of Burgoyne's approach, met him at the head of his camp about three-fourths of a mile south of Fish creek, Burgoyne, in a rich royal uniform, and Gates in a plain blue frock; when they had approached nearly within sword's length, they reined up and halted. The Colonel then named the gentlemen, and General Burgoyne, raising his hat, most gracefully, said, "The fortune of war, General Gates, has made me your prisoner;" to which the conqueror, returning a courtly salute, promptly replied, "I shall always be ready to bear testimony, that it has not been through any fault of your excellency."

Major General Phillips then advanced, and he and General Gates saluted and shook hands with the familiarity of old acquaintances. The Baron Reidesel, and the other officers, were introduced in their turn.

After the introductory ceremony was gone through, Burgoyne, with his general officers, was invited to the head quarters of General Gates, and entertained by him at dinner. They were received with the utmost courtesy, and with the consideration due to brave but unfortunate men. The conversation was unrestrained, affable, and free. Indeed the conduct of General Gates throughout, after the terms of surrender had been adjusted, was marked with equal delicacy and magnanimity, as Burgoyne himself admitted in a letter to the Earl of Derby. In that letter the captive general particularly mentioned one circumstance which, he said, exceeded all he had ever seen or read of on a like occasion. It was the fact, that when the British soldiers had marched out of their camp to the place where they were to pile their arms, *not a man of the American troops was to be seen*—General Gates having ordered his whole army out of sight, that not one of them should be a spectator of the humiliation of the British troops, nor offer the smallest insult to the vanquished. This was a refinement of delicacy and of military generosity and politeness, reflecting the highest credit upon the conqueror; and was spoken of by the officers of Burgoyne in the strongest terms of approbation.

After the British troops left their encampment, and had marched to the "green" in front of Old Fort Hardy,* where they deposited their

---

* Fort Hardy, is a military work thrown up and occupied

arms, and emptied their cartridge boxes; they were again formed in line, with the light infantry in front, and escorted by a company of light dragoons, preceeded by two officers mounted, and bearing the stars and stripes waving triumphantly, through the American camp. On their approach, and as they marched between the long lines of victorious troops, who were then paraded on opposite sides of the road, for near a mile in extent,

> The American Band, with cheerful sound
>   Of sonorous Drum, French horn and Bugle,
> Made the neighboring hills, in joy, resound,
>   To the thund'ring tune of Yankee Doodle!

At this moment the two Generals came out of Gates's marquee together. The American com-

---

by the French, under General Dieskau, in the year 1755. The lines of entrenchment embrace about fifteen acres of ground. The outer works yet retain the appearance of a strong fortification, bounded south by the north side of Fish creek, and east by the right bank of the Hudson. Human bones, fragments of fire-arms, swords, balls, tools, implements, and broken crockery, are frequently picked up on this ground.

In excavating the earth for the Champlain Canal, which passes a few rods west of this Fort, such numbers of human skeletons were found, as made it highly probable this was the cemetery of the French garrison.

mander faced front, and Burgoyne did the same, standing on his left. Not a word was spoken by either, and for some minutes, they stood silently gazing on the scene before them—the one, no doubt, in all the pride of honest success; the other, the victim of regret and sensibility. Burgoyne was a large and stoutly formed man, his countenance was rough and hard, but he had a handsome figure and noble air. Gates was a smaller man, with much less of manner, and destitute of that air which distinguished Burgoyne. Presently General Burgoyne as by previous understanding, stepped back, drew his sword, and in the face of the two armies, as it were, presented it to General Gates, who received and instantly returned it in the most courteous manner. They then returned to the marquee.

The British troops now filed off, with the light infantry still in advance, and the Hessians came lumbering in the rear. Their heavy caps alone were equal to the weight of the whole equipment of a light infantry soldier. It was well known that their services had been sold by their own petty princes, that they were collected together, if not *caught,* at their churches while attending religious worship; and if we may credit the account given us, they were actually torn from their homes and handed over to the British government at so much a head, to be transported across the ocean, and wage war against a people of whose history, and even of whose existence they were ignorant. They were found almost totally unfit for the business they were engaged in. They were unable to march through the woods and encounter the difficulties incident to movements in our then almost unsettled country. Many of them deserted to our army before and after the convention of Saratoga.

Among those German troops, were the Hesse Hanau regiment, Reidesel's dragoons, and Speckt's regiment, the most remarkable of the whole. The officers of distinction who accompanied them, were, Major-General Baron de Reidesel, Quarter-Master-General Gosback, Adjutant-General Poelnic, Secretary Langemegen, Brigadier-General Speckt, Brigadier-General Goll, and some others. The Hessians were extremely dirty in their persons, and had a collection of wild animals in their train—the only thing American they had captured. Here could be seen an artillery-man leading a black grizzly bear, who every now and then would rear upon his hind legs as if he were tired of going upon all fours, or occasionally growl his disapprobation at being pulled along by his chain. In the same manner a tamed deer would be seen tripping lightly after a grenadier. Young foxes were also observed looking sagaciously at the spectators from the top of a baggage wagon, or a young racoon securely clutched under the arm of a sharp shooter. There were a great many women accompanying the Germans, and a miserable looking set of oddly dressed, Gypsey featured females they were.

It is said that no insults were offered to the prisoners as they marched off, and they felt grateful for it. However, after they got out of the camp, many of the British soldiers were extremely abusive, cursing the rebels and their own hard fate. The troops were escorted by some of the New England militia, and crossed the river at Stillwater, on a bridge of rafts, which had been constructed by the Americans while the army were encamped on Bemis's Heights.

On the night of the surrender, a number of Indians and Squaws, the relics of Burgoyne's aboriginal force, were quartered under a strong guard for safe keeping. Without this precaution their lives would not have been safe from the exasperated militia.

The murder of Miss M'Crea was but one of a number of their atrocities, which hardened every heart against them, and prevented the plea of mercy from being interposed in their behalf.

Among these savages were three, that were between six and seven feet in height, perfect giants in form, and possessing the most ferocious countenances. And among them, was recognized the same Indian with whom my father had the encounter at Ensign's.

Blood and carnage were now succeeded by success and plunder. The clouds of battle rolled away, and discovered hundred of searchers after the relics of the tented field.

CHAPTER X

While the British army lay on the north bank of Fish creek, the east side of the river, in addition to the regular troops, was lined with American militia. One of them, an expert swimmer, discovered a number of the enemy's horses feeding in a meadow of General Schuyler's, opposite, and asking permission of his captain to go over and get one of them. It was given, and the man instantly stripped, and swam across the river. He ascended the bank and selecting a fine bay horse for his prize, approached the animal, siezed, and mounted him instantly. This last was the work of a moment. He forced the horse into a gallop, plunged down the bank and brought him safely over to the American camp, although a volley of musketry was fired at him from a party of British soldiers posted at a distance beyond. His success was hailed with enthusiasm, and it had a corresponding effect on his own adventurous spirit. After he had rested himself, he went to his officer and remarked, that it was not proper that a private should ride, whilst his commander went on foot. "So, sir," added he, "if you have no objections, I will go and catch another for you, and next winter when we are home, we will have our own fun in driving a pair of Burgoyne's horses." The captain seemed to think it would be rather a pleasant thing, and gave a ready consent. The fellow actually went across the

BURGOYNE'S CAMPAIGN 225

second time, and with equal success, and brought over a horse that matched exceedingly well with the other. The men enjoyed this prank very much, and it was a circumstance famaliar to almost every one in the army at that time.

Another circumstance happened about the same time, and shows that families were not only divided in feeling on the subject of the war, but that the natural ties which bind the same "kith and kin" together, were not always proof against the political animosities of the times. When Burgoyne found his boats were not safe, and in fact much nearer the main body of the American army than his own, it became necessary to land his provisions, of which he had already been short for many weeks, in order to prevent his army being actually starved into submission. This was done under a heavy fire from the American troops, who were posted on the opposite side of the river. One one of these occasions, a person by the name of Mr. ――――, at Salem, and a foreigner by birth, and who had at the very time a son in the British army, crossed the river at De Ridder's, with a person by the name of M'Niel; they went in a canoe, and arriving opposite to the place intended, crossed over to the western bank, on which a redoubt called Fort Lawrence had been erected. They crawled up the bank with their arms in their hands, and peeping over the upper edge, they saw a man in a blanket coat, loading a cart. They instantly raised their guns to fire, an action more savage than commendable. At the moment the man turned so as to be more plainly seen, old Mr. —— said to his companion, now that's my own son Hughy, but I'll d—'d for a' that if I sill not gi him a shot. He then actually fired at his own son, as the person really proved to be, but happily without effect. Having heard the noise made by their conversation, and the cocking of their pieces, which the nearness of his position rendered perfectly practicable, he ran round the cart, and the balls lodged in the felly of the wheel. The report drew the attention of the neighboring guards, and the two marauders were driven from their lurking place. While retreating with all possible speed M'Niel was wounded in the shoulder, and if alive carries the wound about with him unhealed to this day. Had the ball struck the old Scotchman, it is questionable whether any one would have considered it more than even-handed justice, commending the chalice to his own lips.

At the time Governor George Clinton, to whose indefatigable exertions the state of New-York owes more than she could repay, ordered out the militia of the different counties, and at their head proceeding northwords in hopes of cutting off the retreat of Sir John Johnson, he advanced as far as Crown-Point without meeting the enemy. On his arrival at that post, and hearing nothing of Sir John, my father and John Benson, known and distinguished as *"bare foot Benson,"* who were volunteers at the time, were selected by Governor Clinton, as scouts, to proceed from that post through a dense "howling wilderness," as far as Schroon lake, for the purpose of ascertaining by the "trail" of the Indians, whether Sir John had passed between the two lakes. With only one ration for each, and nothing for their guide but a small pocket compass, they set out with their usual firmness and intrepidity. After travelling over steep and rugged mountains, and through deep, dark, and dismal ravines, they at length reached Schroon lake, without making any discovery, in time to return as far back as the "Beaver Meadows," about two miles west of the head of Brant lake, the first night. During the night, by way of precaution, they deemed it advisable to separate, that, in case they should be discovered by Indians, who were constantly lurking about the country, there might be a better chance, for *one* of them at least, to make his escape and give the alarm. Accordingly they lay down in the tall grass about fifteen or twenty rods apart, for their repose, during the night. About three o'clock in the morning as near as they could judge, they heard a rustling in the grass, about equi-distant from them both, and soon after heard a stepping, like some person cautiously approaching, which they supposed at the time to be the step of some Indian who might have discovered them at the time they conceaued themselves in the grass. On the approach of the object within the circle of their faint vision, they both, as if by concert, though ignorant of each other's intentions, being determined to sell their lives as dear as possible, raised themselves on one knee, levelled their pieces, and fired at the same instant. As soon as they fired, they heard a groan and momentary struggle in the grass, when all again was still as the abodes of death. They then reloaded, and resumed their former positions, but there was no more sleep for them during the remainder of that night. Soon after day break, and when there was light sufficient to discern objects at a distance, they took an observation, and seeing no enemy near, they advanced to ascertain the result of their encounter in the night, when behold, to their surprise, they found they had killed a famous great—deer!

After having their own sport for a while, they started on their return for the camp, by a different route from the one they came, and which they supposed would be nearer, but they had not gone far among the mountains, before the needle to their compass refused to perform its duty, owing no doubt to some neighboring *mineral,* which operated more powerfully than the pole. After wandering about for some time, in a dark and dismal forest, it being a dark and cloudy day, they became bewildered and finally got lost. Thus they continued to travel through the day, and found themselves at night near the place where they started from in the morning. By this time, having fasted twenty-four hours, their appetites became so sharp they thought they would make a meal out of the deer they had fortuitously killed the night before; but on their arrival at the spot they found that the wolves or some other animals had devoured it, and left not even a bone. They then laid themselves down for repose, on the same bed of grass they had occupied the night of the encounter. The next morning they again started for the camp, by the same route they came the first day, though somewhat faint for the want of food. About ten o'clock they came across a knapsack, which had been lost or left in the woods, by some person to them unknown, containing a lot of boiled pork, bread and cheese promiscuously thrown in together, and out of which Benson made a hearty meal; but my father, having so strong an aversion even to the *smell* of cheese that he refused to taste a mouthful of any of the contents of the knapsack; and accordingly stood it out until he arrived at camp, about three o'clock in the afternoon of the third day, where they were received, with much joy, by the Governor and his staff, who had given them up for lost. It was thus ascertained that Sir John, with his horde of Indians, had not retreated in that direction, and the Governor gave up all hopes of intercepting them on this occasion, and returned home.

> The Savage comes, the spoiler of your land,
> With all his howling, desolating band;
> Red is the cup they drink, but not with wine;
> Watch then to-night, or see no morning shine!

As I have pledged myself, in my introduction, to give all the principal facts connected with Burgoyne's campaign, as far as they have come to my knowledge, and as I am not writing to please any particular individual or class of readers, I will relate the following incident, which is often spoken of even to this day.

The inhabitants throughout this part of the country, having been much harrassed by the Indians and Tories, and in constant danger of their lives, were consequently under the necessity, for their own safety, of building, at different stations, what they termed Block-houses.

These buildings were constructed of logs flattened on two sides and locked or halved together at the angles or corners, which rendered them strong and proof against rifle or musket balls. On each side about six feet from the bottom was an interstice or narrow space between the logs, for the purpose, in case of a siege or an attack, of thrusting their guns through to fire on the besiegers. Below this open space a platform was erected about two feet from the floor, to stand upon while firing. The buildings were constructed without windows, and with but one door, which was made strong, and when occupied, was strongly barricaded. To these buildings, when it was known or suspected there were Indians or Tories in the vicinity, a number of families would resort during the night, leaving their own dwellings much exposed, and many of which were plundered and consumed.

The block-houses were often attacked, and sometimes with considerable force, but as near as I have been able to learn, without much success, though with some loss to the assailants.

It happened during a considerable interval of time, in which no Indians had been seen in the neighborhood, that the inhabitants ceased resorting to their block-houses. At this time a man by the name of Joseph Seely, whose vicious habits generally led him more to the gratification of his own evil propensities, than the public weal, and who had been out one day on a hunting excursion, for which he was very famous, and not very fastidious about the kind of game he "bagged," even if it was a turkey or a fowl that might *accidentally* come in his way, returned from the woods, saying he had come across a party of Indians and Tories, at whom he had fired, and as he thought, killed one. The alarm was immediately spread throughout the neighborhood, and the men all armed themselves, and flocked together, for the purpose of going in pursuit. On being led by Seely to the place where he said he had shot at the Indians, they found a trail of blood extending some distance through the woods, which led them on the course they concluded it best to pursue, not doubting, from the circumstances of the blood, that he had severely wounded, if not killed one of the Indians or Tories.

After traveling some miles and finding no enemy, they concluded they might have secreted themselves in the neighborhood, with the intention of committing their savage deeds during the following night. Accordingly they all returned home, it being near night, and for safety, after secreting as much of their effects as they conveniently could, they and their families resorted to their block-houses, and by turns watch for the enemy during the night; but none appeared to molest them.

The next morning they very cautiously returned to their several homes, and many of them with the expectation of finding their property destroyed, and their dwellings in ashes. About ten o'clock, this mischief-bent hero of the forest, after having his own sport at the expense of his neighbors, and feeling conscious he had carried the joke rather too far, finally disclosed the whole secret. Having spent the whole forenoon of the previous day, and finding no game, on his return came across a flock of sheep, and from his natural propensity to mischief, he fired among them, and badly wounded one, when they all ran into the woods. On pursuing them some distance to see if the wounded sheep died, he observed the blood trickled along on the leaves; upon which he thought he would raise a "hue and cry," and alarm the neighborhood, by the horrible story he told of having seen and shot an Indian.

The following daring fete was performed by the author's great-uncle, Captain Hezekiah Dunham, who commanded a militia company in the vicinity of Bemis's Heights, a staunch whig, and a firm friend to the American cause.

One evening as he was at a public entertainment, a boy was seen emerging from the woods in the neighborhood on horseback, and presently approaching the place where the people were collected, asked if he could purchase a little rum. When he was answered no, he immediately mounted, returned a considerable distance, and then we seen galloping down the main road by the river. On seeing this, Dunham exclaimed, "This means something, I am sure of it." He then watched for the boy's return, and in a few minutes he repassed at full speed. He then reentered the wood, and was gone from their sight in an instant. Dunham's penetration induced him to say, "The enemy is near us: the Tories are in our neighborhood, and not far off." He separated from his company, with a determination to act immediately.

Dunham, when he reached home, immediately went to a person by the name of Green, who was a son of Vulcan and of Mars, and an able-bodied, bold and persevering fellow. He was the pride of his settlement, and the safeguard of the people around him—always ready for action, never desponding, and fearless to an extent that was remarkable. He was always relied upon in trying emergencies by the leading men in the vicinity, and what completed his merits, he was never backward. Dunham related the circumstance to him, and declared his belief that there was a party of Tories in the neighborhood.

Three other persons were called upon the same night for assistance, and when the rest of their neighbors were asleep, these hardy men commenced their reconnosance. Every suspected spot was carefully approached in hopes of finding the objects of their search. Every hollow that could contain a hiding place was looked into; but in a more particular manner the out-houses and barns of those persons who were suspected for their attachment to the enemy, were examined by them. It seemed all in vain. No traces of a concealed foe were discovered, when towards day-break it was proposed to separate and make one final search for that time. Dunham took two men with him, and Green but one. The former, as a last effort returned to the house of one ———, who it was probable would be in communication with an enemy if near him. As he approached the house he had to pass a meadow adjoining, and observed a path leading from the house to a small thicket of about three acres in extent. Dunham immediately suspected it led to his enemy. He pursued it, and found it passed around the thicket, and when it almost met the place where it turned off, the path entered the wood. Dunham paused, and turning to his companions said, "Here they are, will you follow me?" They instantly moved to accompany him, and the party moved on in single file, with light and cautious steps. As they got nearly to the center, Dunham in advance, a log stopped up the path, and seemed to prevent any farther approach. With a motion that indicated the necessity of their remaining still, he mounted the log, and looking over, discovered, sure enough, at once a desired and yet imposing sight. Around the remains of a watch-fire, which day-break rendered less necessary, sat a group of five fierce looking men, with countenances relaxed from their usual fixedness; but yet betokening boldness, if not savageness of purpose. They were dressing themselves, and putting on their shoes and stockings, which stood beside their rude couches. Their clothes were much worn, but had a military cut, which making their stout and muscular forms more apparent, gave them a peculiar snug fit, and distinguished them from the loose, slovenly scarecrow figures which the homely character of our country seamstresses impossed upon everything rural or rusticated among our people. Their hats or caps were set carelessly on their heads, with the air of regulars; and what made them still more observed was, that every man of them had his musket at his side on the ground, ready to be used at an instant's notice. Dunham surveyed this scene a few moments, and then drew back cautiously to his companions. In a tone not above a whisper, he said, "Shall we take 'em!" A nod from his companions decided him—each now examined his musket, and reprimed it. The captain took the right of his little band, and they moved forward to the log. They mounted it at the same instant, and as they did so, Dunham cried out, "surrender or you are all dead men!" The group that thus found themselves almost under the "muzzles of their enemies' guns," were indeed astonished. All but their leader, Thomas Lovelass, seemed petrified and motionless. This resolute man seemed disposed to make an effort for their lives. Twice amid the silence and stillness of the perilous moment, he stretched out his hand to seize his gun. Each time he was prevented by the near approach of the muzzle that pointed at his head, and beyond which he saw an unflinching eye steadfastly fixed upon him; at the same instant he was told, that if he touched it he was a dead man.

At this critical period of the rencontre, Dunham peremptorily ordered the party to come out, one by one, which they reluctantly did, fearing perhaps that they were surrounded by and in contact with a superior force. As fast as one came over the log he was secured by the most powerful man of the three, while the other two kept their pieces steadily pointed at the prisoners. Some young women who proved to be sisters of some of the party, gave way to the most violent grief. Well aware of the danger they were in, and the speedy vengeance inflicted upon Tories and spies, they anticipated the most dreadful consequences to their unhappy brothers, and no words can express the frantic sorrow to which they abandoned themselves. The young men themselves assumed an air of firmness, but it was easily penetrated. They confessed that their intention was to capture and take off some of the most active Whigs in the neighborhood. One of the prisoners upon promise of quarters, informed that he belonged to a party of fifteen, who had come down from Canada on the same business—who were then in various disguises, scattered through the country to ascertain the state of affairs for the benefit of the British general in Canada, who was planning an inroad, and that they had left their boats concealed on the shores of Lake George. The country was at that time overrun with spies and traitors. Robberies were frequent, and the inhabitants, (non combatants) carried prisoners to Canada. General Schuyler's house was robbed and two of his servants, or life-guards carried there. The general saved himself by retiring to his chamber, barricading the door, and firing upon the marauders.

Lovelass and his companions, were taken to the barracks at Saratoga, where they were tried and condemned to court-martial, of which the celebrated General Stark was president. Lovelass alone suffered death. He was considered too dangerous a man to be permitted to escape. He complained that being found with arms in his hands, he was only a prisoner, and many thought that such being the fact, he was scarcely punishable as a spy. Indeed he even bewailed his hard fate, and the injustice done him, but found he had nothing to expect from the judges. In two or three days he was brought out of his place of confinement, and suffered death upon the gallows, during a tremendous storm of rain and wind, accompanied with heavy and often repeated claps of thunder, and the most vivid flashes of lightning.

I have adverted but little to the sufferings of the American army, because but little comparatively, is known of what they individually endured. Excepting the inevitable casualties of battle, they must have suffered much less than their enemies; for they soon ceased to be the flying, and because the attacking and triumphant party. Colonels Colburn, Adams, Francis, and many other brave officers and men, gave up their lives, as the price of their country's liberty, and very many carried away with them the scars produced by honorable wounds.

The bravery of the American army was fully acknowledged by their adversaries. "At all times," said Lord Balcarras, "when I was opposed to the rebels, they fought with great courage and obstinacy. We were taught by experience, that neither their attacks nor resistance was to be despised. Speaking of the retreat of the Americans at Ticonderoga, and of their behaviour at the battle of Hubbarton, Lord Balcarras adds: "circumstanced as the enemy were, as an army very hard pressed in their retreat, they certainly behaved with great gallantry; of the attack on the lines, on the evening of the 7th October, he says—The lines were attacked, and with as much fury as the fire of small arms can admit.

Captain Mooney, in answer to the questions whether on the 19th of September the Americans disputed the field with obstinacy, answered, they did, and the fire was much hotter than I ever knew it anywhere, except at the affair at Fort Ann; and speaking of the battle of October 7th, and of the moment when the Americans, with nothing but small arms, were marching up to the British artillery, he adds, I was very much astonished to hear the shot from the enemy fly so thick after our cannonade had lasted a quarter of an hour.

General Burgoyne gives it as his opinion,

that as rangers, perhaps there are few better in the world, than the corps of Virginia riflemen which acted under Colonel Morgan. He says, speaking of the battle of September 19th, that few actions have been characterized by more obstinacy, in attack or defence. The British bayonet was repeatedly tried ineffectually.

Remarking upon the battle of the 7th of October, he observes: If there be any persons who continue to doubt that the Americans possess the *quality* and *faculty* of fighting, call it by whatever term you please, they are of a prejudice, that it would be very absurd longer to contend with; he says, that in his action the British troops retreated hard pressed, but in good order, and that the troops had hardly entered the camp, when it was stormed with great fury—the enemy rushing to the lines, under a severe fire of grape-shot and small arms.

It is very gratifying to every real American to find, that for so great a prize, his countrymen, (their enemies themselves being judges) contended so nobly, and that their conduct for bravery, skill and humanity, will stand the scrutiny of all future ages.

From the enemy it becomes us not to withhold the commendation that is justly due; all that skill and valor could effect, they accomplished, and they were overwhelmed at last by complicated distresses, and by superior numbers.

The vaunting proclamation of Burgoyne, at the commencement of the campaign; some of his boasting letters, written during the progress of it, and his devastation of private property, reflect no honor on his memory. But in general, he appears to have been a humane and honorable man, a scholar and a gentleman, a brave soldier and an able commander. Some of his sentiments have a higher moral tone than is common with men of his profession, and have probably procured for him more respect, than all his battles. Speaking of the battle of the 7th, he says: In the course of the action, a shot had passed through my hat, and another had passed through my waistcoat. I should be sorry to be thought, at any time, insensible to the protecting hand of Providence; but I never, more particularly considered (and I hope not superstitiously) a soldier's hair breath escapes as incentives to duty a *marked renewal of the trust of being,* for the purposes of a public station: and under that reflection, to loose our fortitude, by giving way to our affections; to be divested by any possible self-emotion from meeting a present exigency, with our best faculties, were at once dishonor and impiety.

Thus have I adverted to some of the leading circumstances of the greatest military event which has ever occurred in America; but compared with the whole extent and diversity of that campaign, the above notices however extended, are few and brief. Should the notice of these great events tend, in any instance, to quench the odious fires of party, and rekindle those of genuine patriotism—should it revive in any one a veneration for the virtues of those men who faced death, in every form, regardless of their own lives, and bent only on securing to posterity the precious blessings which we now enjoy; and above all, should we thus be led to cherish a higher sense of gratitude to heaven for our unexampled privileges, and to use them more temperately and wisely, the time occupied in this narrative, will not have been spent in vain. History presents no struggle for liberty which has in it more of the moral sublime than that of the American Revolution. It has been, of late years, too much forgotten in the sharp contentions of party, and he who endeavors to withdraw the public mind from those debasing conflicts, and to fix it on the grandeur of that great epoch—which, magnificent in itself, begins now *to wear the solemn livery of antiquity, as it is viewed through the deepening twilight of more than half a century,* certainly performs a meritorious service, and can scarcely need a justification.

The generation that sustained the conflict, is now almost passed away; a few hoary heads remain seamed with honorable scars—a very few *experienced* guides can still attend us to the fields of carnage, and point out the places where they and their companions fought and bled, and where now sleep the bones of the slain. But these men will soon be gone; tradition and history, will however, continue to recite their deeds, and the latest generations will be taught to venerate the defenders of our liberties; to visit the "memorable battle grounds," which were moistened with their blood, and to thank the mighty God of battles that the arduous conflict terminated in the entire establishment of the liberties of this country.

TO THE READER

It was the author's intention at the commencement of this "narrative," to have given credit for such matter as he might be induced to draw from other sources than those named in the introduction. But in the progress of his writing, he found his own corrections and remarks, in many instances, so commingled with those selections, as to render it almost, if not not quite, impracticable, and possibly so unintelligible to many, that he was reluctantly compelled to abandon the idea in many cases. And to give credit in one instance and not in another, would manifestly be doing an injustice; he has therefore left it for the reader to make his own researches, as a means of improving his habits of reading, and possibly, his understanding. In the meantime the author apologizes to those from whom he has, more or less, drawn, believing, as his object is to give a correct statement of facts, they will deem it of sufficient credit to them, to know that they have been referred to as authority for a portion of this work.

APPENDIX.

The following is an extract of a letter written by the venerable Samuel Woodruff, Esq., of Connecticut, a volunteer under Gen. Gates, and a participator in the battle of the seventh of October, and who again visited the very important ground some few years since.

In speaking of his tour to Stillwater and Saratoga to gratify a desire he had felt, and which had long been increasing, to view the battle grounds at that place, and the spot on which the royal army under the command of General Burgoyne surrendered to General Gates, on the 17th October, 1777, he says:

"You will excuse me for entering a little into the feelings of Uncle Toby respecting Dendermond in the compressed and hastily written journal I kept of my tour, especially as you will take into consideration that I had the honor to serve as a volunteer under General Gates part of that campaign, and was in the battle of the 7th of October.

"I take the liberty to enclose to you an extract of that part of my journal which embraces the principal object of my tour.

"At 7 A. M. started on foot to view some other equally interesting places connected with the campaign of 1777, three (six) miles and a half south of Fish creek, called at the house of a Mr. Smith, in which General Frazer died of wounds received in the battle of the 7th of October, and near which house in one of the British redoubts, that officer was buried. This house (owned at the time by John Taylor, of Albany,) then stood by the road on the west margin of the interval, at the foot of the rising ground. A turnpike road having since been constructed, running twenty or thirty rods east of the old road, the latter has been discontinued, and Mr. Smith (Lee,) has drawn the house and placed it on the west side of the turnpike.

"Waiving, for the present, any farther notices of this spot, I shall attempt a concise narrative of the two hostile armies for a short period anterior to the great battle of the 7th of October.

"The object of the British General was to penetrate as far as Albany, at which place, by concert, he was to meet Sir Henry Clinton, then with a fleet and army at New-York. In the early part of September, General Burgoyne had advanced with his army from Fort Edward, and crossed the Hudson with his artillery, baggage wagons, &c., on a bridge of boats, and entrenched the troops on the highlands of Saratoga (Stillwater). On the 19th of September they left their entrenchments, and moved south by a slow and cautious march towards the American camp, which was secured by a line of entrenchments and redoubts on Bemis's Heights, running from west to east about half a mile in length, terminating at the east on the west side of the interval.

"Upon the approach of the royal army, the American forces sallied forth from their camp, and met the British about a mile north of the American lines. A severe conflict ensued, and many brave officers and men fell on both sides. The ground on which this battle was fought was principally covered with standing wood. This circumstance somewhat embarrassed the British troops in the use of their field artillery, and afforded some advantage to the Americans, particularly the riflemen under the command of the brave Colonel Morgan, who did great execution. Night, which has often and so kindly interposed to stop the carnage of conflicting hosts, put an end to the battle.

"Neither party claimed a victory. The royal army withdrew in the night, leaving the field and their slain with some of their wounded in possession of the Americans. The loss of killed and wounded, as near as could be ascertained, was, on the part of the British, six hundred; and on that of the Americans about three hundred and fifty. The bravery and firmness of the American forces displayed this day, convinced the British officers of the difficulty if not utter impossibility of continuing their march to Albany. The season for closing the campaign in that northern region was advancing—the American army was daily augmenting by militia, volunteers and the "two months' men," as they were called. The fear that the two royal armies might effect their junction at Albany, aroused the neighboring states of New-England, and drew from New-Hampshire, Massachusetts, Connecticut and Vermont, a large body of determined soldiers. Baum's defeat at Bennington had inspired them with new hopes and invigorated their spirits.

"Under these circumstances, inauspicious to the hostile army, the British commander-in-chief summoned a council of war; the result of which was to attempt a retreat across the Hudson to Fort Edward. General Gates, apprehending the probability of this measure, seasonably detached a portion of his force to intercept and cut off the retreat should that be attempted.

"Many new and unexpected difficulties now presented themselves. The boats which had served the British army for a bridge, being considered by them as of no further use, had been cut loose, and most of them floated down the river. The construction of rafts sufficient for conveying over their artillery and heavy baggage, would be attended with great danger as well as loss of time. The bridges over the creeks had been destroyed; great quantities of trees had been felled across the roads by order of the American general; and another thing, not of the most trifling nature, Fort Edward was already in possession of the Americans. In this perplexing dilemma the royal army found themselves completely *checkmated*. A retreat, however, was attempted, but soon abandoned. Situated as they now were, between two fires, every motion they made was fraught with danger and loss, they retired to their old entrenched camp.

"Several days elapsed without any very active operations on either side. This interval of time, was, however, improved by the royal army in preparations to make one desperate effort to force the lines of the American camp, and cut their way through on their march to Albany. The American army improved the meantime in strengthening their outer works, arranging their forces, and placing the continentals on the north side of the entrenchments, where valiant men were expected; thus preparing to defend every point of attack. Morgan, with his riflemen, to form the left flank in the woods.

"During these few days of 'dreadful preparation,' information daily arrived in our camp, by deserters and otherwise, that an attack would soon be made upon the line of our entrenchments at Bemis's Heights near the head quarters of General Gates.

"The expected conflict awakened great anxiety among the American troops, but abated nothing of that stirling intrepidity and firmness which they uniformly displayed in the hour of danger; all considered that the expected conflict would be decisive of the campaign at least, if not of the war in which we had been so long engaged. Immense interests were at stake. Should General Burgoyne succeed in marching his army to Albany, General Clinton, without any considerable difficulty, would there join him with another powerful English army, and a fleet sufficient to command the Hudson from thence to New-York. Should this junction of force take place, all the states east of the Hudson would be cut off from all efficient communication with the western and southern states.

"In addition to this there were other considerations of the deepest concern. The war had already been protracted to a greater length of time than was expected on either side at the commencement. The resources of the country, which were at first comparatively small in respect to those things necessary for war, began to fail; the term of enlistment of many of the soldiers had expired.

"We had no public money, and no government to guarantee the payment of wages to the officers and soldiers, nor to those who furnished supplies for the troops. Under these discouraging circumstances it became extremely difficult to raise recruits for the army. During the year 1776, and the fore part of '77, the Americans suffered greatly by sickness, and were unsuccessful in almost every rencontre with the enemy. Men's hearts, even the stoutest, began to fail. This was indeed the most gloomy period of the war of the Revolution.

"On the 7th of October, about ten o'clock A. M., the royal army commenced their march, and formed their line of battle on our left, near Bemis's Heights, with General Frazer at their head. Our pickets were driven in about one o'clock P. M., and were followed by the British troops on a quick march to within fair musket shot distance of the line of our entrenchments. At this moment commenced a tremendous discharge of cannon and musketry, which was returned with equal spirit by the Americans.

"For thirty or forty minutes the struggle at the

breast-works was maintained with great obstinacy. Several charges with fixed bayonets were made by the English grenadiers with but little effect. Great numbers fell on both sides. The ardor of this bloody conflict continued for some time without any apparent advantage gained by either party. At length, however, the assailants began to give way, preserving good order in a regular but slow retreat—loading, wheeling and firing, with considerable effect. The Americans followed up the advantage they had gained, by a brisk and well directed fire of field pieces and musketry. Colonel Morgan with his riflemen hung upon the left wing of the retreating enemy, and galled them by a most destructive fire. The line of battle now became extensive, and most of the troops of both armies were brought into action. The principal part of the ground on which this hard day's work was done, is known by the name of Freeman's Farm. It was then covered by a thin growth of pine wood without underbrush, except one lot of about six or eight acres which had been cleared and fenced. On this spot the British grenadiers, under the command of the brave Major Ackland, made a stand, and brought together some of their field artillery; this little field soon became literally 'the field of blood.' These grenadiers, the flower of the royal army, unaccustomed to yield to any opposing force in fair field, fought with that obstinate spirit which borders on madness. Ackland received a ball through both legs, which rendered him unable to walk or stand. This occurrence hastened the retreat of the grenadiers, leaving the ground thickly strewed with dead and wounded.

"The battle was continued by a brisk running fire until dark. The victory was complete; leaving the Americans masters of the field. Thus ended a battle of the highest importance in its consequences, and added great lustre to the American arms—I have seen no official account of the numbers killed and wounded; but the loss on the part of the British must have been great, and that on the Americans not inconsiderable. The loss of general officers suffered by the royal army was peculiarly severe.

"But to return to the Smith house. For several days previous to that time, General Burgoyne had made that house his head-quarters, accompanied by several general officers and their ladies, among whom were General Frazer, the Baron and Baroness Reidesel, and their children.

"The circumstances attending the fall of this gallant officer have presented a question about which military men are divided in opinion. The facts seem to be agreed, that soon after the commencement of the action, General Arnold, knowing the military character and efficiency of General Frazer, and observing his motions in leading and conducting the attack, said to Colonel Morgan, "That officer upon a grey horse is of himself a host, and must be disposed of—direct the attention of some of the sharp-shooters among your riflemen to him." Morgan nodding his assent to Arnold, repaired to his riflemen, and made known to them the hint given by Arnold. Immediately upon this, the crupper of the grey horse was cut off by a rifle bullet, and within the next minute another passed through the horse's mane, a little back of his ears. An aid of Frazer noticing this, observed to him, "Sir, it is evident that you are marked out for particular aim; would it not be prudent for you to retire from this place?" Frazer replied, "my duty forbids me to fly from danger," and immediately received a bullet through his body. A few grenadiers were detached to carry him to the Smith (Taylor) house.

"Having introduced the name of Arnold, it may be proper to note here, that although he had no regular command that day, he volunteered his service, was early on the ground, and in the hottest part of the struggle at the redoubts. He behaved (as I then thought,) more like a mad-man than a cool and discreet officer. Mounted on a brown horse, he moved incessantly on a full gallop back and forth, until he received a wound in his leg and his horse was shot under him. I happened to be near him when he fell, and assisted in getting him into a litter to be carried to headquarters.

"Late in the evening Burgoyne came in, and a tender scene took place between him and Frazer. General Frazer was the idol of the British army, and the officer on whom, of all others, Burgoyne placed the greatest reliance. He languished through the night, and expired at eight o'clock the next morning. While on his death-bed he advised Burgoyne, without delay, to propose to General Gates terms of capitulation, and prevent the further effusion of blood; that the situation of his army was now hopeless; they could neither advance nor retreat. He also requested that he might be buried in the *great redout,* his body to be borne thither between sunset and dark, by a body of the grenadiers, without parade or ceremony. This request was strictly complied with.

"After viewing the house to my satisfaction, I walked up to the place of interment. It is situated on an elevated piece of ground, commanding an extensive view of the Hudson, and a great length of the beautiful interval on each side of it. I was alone; the weather was calm and serene. Reflections were awakened in my mind which I am wholly unable to describe. Instead of the bustle and hum of the camp, and confused noise of the battle of the warrior, and the shouts of victory which I here witnessed more than fifty years ago, all was now silent as the abodes of the dead. And indeed far, far the greatest part of both those armies who was then in active life, at and near this spot, are now mouldering in their graves, like that valiant officer whose remains are under my feet, "their memories and their names lost," while God, in his merciful providence, has preserved my life, and after the lapse of more than half a century, has afforded me an opportunity of once more viewing those places, which force upon my mind interesting recollections of my youthful days."

The Baroness de Reidesel in speaking of the movements of Burgoyne's army, says, when the army broke up (at Batten kill,) on the eleventh of September,

1777, she was at first told that she must remain behind; but on her repeated entreaties, and as other ladies had been permitted to follow the army, the same indulgence was extended to her. They advanced by short journeys, and went through many toils; yet she would have purchased at any price the privilege thus granted to her of daily seeing her husband. She had sent back her baggage, and only kept a small bundle of summer dresses. In the beginning all went well; they thought that there was little doubt of their being successful, and of reaching *"the promised land;"* and when on the passage across the Hudson, General Burgoyne exclaimed, "Britons never retrograde," their spirits rose mightily. She observed, however, with suspicion, that the wives of the officers were beforehand informed of all the military plans; and she was so much the more struck with it, as she remembered with how much secrecy all dispositions were made in the armies of Duke Ferdinand during the seven years' war. Thus the Americans anticipated their movements, and expected them wherever they arrived; and this of course injured their affairs. On the ninteenth of September, an action took place which ended, she says, to their advantage; but they were in consequence, obliged to halt at a place called Freeman's farm. She witnessed the whole action, and knowing that her husband was among the cambatants, she was full of anxiety and trembled at every shot—nothing escaped her ear. She saw a great number of wounded, and what was still worse, three of them were brought into the house where she was. One of them was a Major Harnage, whose wife was with them; the second a lieutenant, whose wife was of her acquaintance; and the third a young English officer, called Young. The Major occupied, with his wife, a room close by where she was. He had received a shot through his body, and suffered exquisite pain. A few days after their arrival, she heard groans in another room, and was told that the young officer, whom she had just mentioned, was lying there, and that his recovery was very doubtful. She took much interest in him, as a family of his name had shown her great kindness during her stay in England. He expressed a great desire to see his benefactress, for so he called her. She went into his room and found him on a thin bed of straw, for he had lost all his baggage. He was eighteen or nineteen years old, an only son, and a nephew of the same Mr. Young she had known in England. He lamented for his parents' sake, but said nothing of his sufferings. He had lost much blood, and the surgeon advised him to submit to the amputation of his leg; but he would not consent to it, though the limb had become gangrenous. She sent him pillows and blankets, and her maids gave him their mattress. She took more and more care of him, and visited him daily; for which he thanked her a thousand times. At last the amputation took place; but it was too late, and he died a few days afterwards. Her room being close to his, and the walls very thin, she heard his last moans.

For their further march, she had caused a calash to be made for her, in which she could take not only her children, but also her two female attendants; and thus she followed the army in the midst of the troops who were in great spirits, and sang and longed for victory.

They marched, she says, through endless forests, and a beautiful district, though deserted by the inhabitants, who ran away at their approach to reinforce General Gates's army. They are naturally soldiers and excellent marksmen, and the idea of fighting for their country and their liberty increased their innate courage. Her husband was encamped with the rest of the army; being herself an hour's ride behind the army, she went every morning to pay him a visit in the camp, and sometimes she dined there with him, but generally he took his dinner at her quarters. There was daily skirmishes with the enemy, generally of little importance. But her husband could never sleep without his clothes. The weather already having grown rougher, Colonel Williams of the artillery, thought their mutual visits were rather too fatiguing for them, and proposed to have a house built for her with a chimney, which should not cost more than five or six guineas, and which she could uninterruptedly inhabit. She accepted of his offer, and the building, which was to be about twenty feet square, was begun. Such a dwelling is called a block house, for which logs nearly of equal diameter are put together; if the interstices are filled up with clay, it is not only very solid, but very warm. She was to take possession of it on the next day; and she rejoiced in it the more, she says, as the nights were damp and cold, and it being close to the camp, her husband would be able to be with her. But severe trials awaited them, and on the seventh of October, their misfortunes began. She was at breakfast with her husband, and heard that something was intended. On the same day she expected Generals Burgoyne, Phillips, and Frazer, to dine with her. She saw a great movement among the troops and inquired the cause; her husband told her it was merely a reconnoisance, which gave her no concern, as it often happened. She walked out of the house and met several Indians in their war dresses, with guns in their hands. When she asked them where they were going; they cried out, "War! War!" (meaning they were going to battle.) This filled her with apprehension, and she scarcely got home before she heard reports of cannon and musketry, which grew louder by degrees, till at last the noise became excessive. About four o'clock in the afternoon, instead of the guests whom she expected, General Frazer was brought on a litter mortally wounded. The table which was already set, was instantly removed and a bed placed in its stead for the wounded general. She sat trembling in a corner; the noise grew louder, and the alarm increased; the thought that her husband might perhaps be brought in wounded in the same way, was terrible to her, and distressed her exceedingly. General Frazer said to the surgeon, "Tell *me if my wound is mortal; do not flatter me."* The ball had passed through his body, and unhappily for the general, he had eaten a very hearty breakfast, by which the stomach was distended, and the ball, as the surgeon said, had passed through it. She heard him often exclaim with a sigh, "Oh, fatal ambition! Poor General Burgoyne! Oh my poor wife!" He was asked if he had any request to make; to which he replied, that "If General Burgoyne would permit it, he should like to be buried at six o'clock in the evening on the top of a hill, on a redoubt which had been built there. She says she did not know which way to turn, all the other rooms were full of sick. Towards evening she saw her husband coming; then she forgot all her sorrows, and thanked God that he was spared to her. He ate in great haste with her and his aid-de-camp behind the house. She had been told that they had the advantage of the enemy, but the sorrowful faces she beheld told a different tale, and before her husband went away, he took her one side and said every thing was going very bad, that she must keep herself in readiness to leave the place, but not to mention it to any one. She made the pretence that she would move the next morning into her new house, and had every thing packed up ready.

Lady Harriet Ackland had a tent not far from her house; in this she slept, and the rest of the day she was in the camp. All of a sudden a man came to tell her that her husband was mortally wounded, and taken prisoner; on hearing this she became very miserable; the Baroness comforted her by telling her that the wound was only slight, and at the same time advised her to go over to her husband, to do which, she would certainly obtain permission, and then she could attend to him herself; she was a charming woman and very fond of him. The Baroness spent much of the night in comforting her, and then went again to her children whom she had put to bed. She could not go to sleep, as she had General Frazer and all the other wounded gentlemen in her room, and she was sadly afraid her children would awake, and by their crying disturb the dying man in his last moments, who often addressed her, and apologized *"for the trouble he gave her."* About 3 o'clock in the morning she was told he could not hold out much longer; she had desired to be informed of the near approach of this sad crisis, and she then wrapped up her children in their clothes, and went with them into the room below. About 8 o'clock in the morning he died. After he was laid out and his corpse wrapped up in a sheet, she came again into the room, and had this sorrowful sight before her the whole day; and to add to this melancholy scene, almost every moment, some officer of her acquaintance was brought in wounded. The cannonade commenced again; a retreat was spoken of, but not the smallest motion was made towards it. About 4 o'clock in the afternoon she saw the house which had just been built for her in flames, and the enemy was now not far off. They knew that General Burgoyne would not refuse the last request of General Frazer, though by his acceding an unnecessary delay was occasioned by which the inconvenience of the army was much increased. At 6 o'clock the corps was brought out, and she saw all the generals attend it to the hill; the chaplain, Mr. Brudenell, performed the funeral service, rendered unusually solemn and awful, from its being accompanied by constant peals from the American artillery. Many cannon balls flew close by her; but she had her eyes directed towards the hill, where her husband was standing amid the fire of the Americans, and of course, she could not think of her own danger. She says General Gates afterwards said, that if he had known it had been a funeral, he would not have permitted it to be fired on.

Orders had already been issued that the army should break up immediately after the funeral, and their calashes were got ready. She was unwilling to depart sooner. Major Harnage, though hardly able to walk a step, left his bed, that he might not remain in the hospital, upon which a flag of truce had been erected. When he saw the Baroness there in the midst of danger, he drove her children and female attendants into the vehicle, and told her that she had not a moment to lose. She begged to be permitted to remain a little longer. "Do what you please," replied he,—"but your children I must at least save." This touched her most tender feelings: she sprang into the carriage, and at eight o'clock they departed.

The Baroness Reidesel further says, they were halted at six o'clock in the morning at Do-ve-gat, to their great amazement. At length, however, they recommenced their march, and arrived at Saratoga on the ninth, about dark; which was but half an hour's march from the place where they spent the day. She was quite wet, and was obliged to remain in that condition for want of a place to change her apparel. She seated herself near the fire and undressed the children, and they then laid themselves upon some straw. She asked General Phillips, who came to see how she was, why they did not continue their retreat, her husband having pledged himself to cover the movement, and to bring off the army in safety. "My poor lady," said he, you astonish me. Though quite wet, you have so much courage as to wish to go further in this weather. What a pity it is that you are not our commanding general! He complains of fatigue, and has determined upon spending the night here, and giving us a supper." It is very true that General Burgoyne liked to make himself easy, and that he spent half his nights in singing and drinking, and diverting himself with the wife of a commissary, who was his mistress and who was as fond of champaign as himself.

The Baronness refreshed herself at 7 o'clock the next morning, (the 10th of October) with a cup of tea, and they all expected that they should soon continue their march. General Burgoyne had given orders to set fire to General Schuyler's fine buildings and mills at Saratoga, for the purpose of securing their retreat. An English officer brought her some good soup, and insisted that she should partake of it. After this they continued their march, but only for a short time. There was much misery and disorder in the army. The commissaries had forgotten to distribute provisions, though they had an abundance of cattle. She says she saw more than thirty officers who complained bitterly of hunger. She gave them coffee and tea, and every thing eatable she had in her calash. Their calashes remained in readiness to depart. Every body advised a retreat, and her husband pledged himself to effect that movement, if no time was lost. But General Burgoyne, who was promised an *order* if he should effect his junction with General Howe, could not be persuaded to it, and lost every thing by his dilatoriness.

About two o'clock they heard again a report of muskets and cannon, and there was much alarm and bustle among their troops. Her husband sent her word that she should immediately retire into a house (now occupied by Mrs. Bushee) not far off. She got into her calash with her children; and when they were near the house, she saw, on the opposite bank of the Hudson, five or six men, who aimed at them with their guns. Without knowing what she did, she threw her children into the back part of the calash, and laid herself upon them. At the same moment the fellows fired and broke the arm of a poor English soldier, who stood behind her, and who, being already wounded, sought a shelter. Soon after their arrival a terrible cannonade began, and the fire was principally directed against the house, where she had hoped to find a refuge, probably because the enemy inferred, from the great number of people who went towards it, that this was the head quarters of the generals, while in reality none were there except women and crippled soldiers. She says, they were at last obliged to descend into the cellar, where she laid herself in a corner near the door. Her children put their heads upon her knees. An abominable smell, the cries of the children, and her own anguish of mind did not permit her eyes to close during the whole night.

On the next morning the cannonade began anew,

but in a different direction. She advised her fellow sufferers to withdraw for a while from the cellar, in order to give time to clean it, for they should otherwise injure their health. On an inspection of their retreat, she discovered that there were three cellars, spacious and well vaulted. She suggested that one of them should be appropriated to the use of the officers, who were most severely wounded, and the next to the females, and the third, which was nearest to the staircase, to all the rest of the company. They were just going down, when a new thunder of cannon threw them again into alarm. Many persons who had no right to enter, threw themselves against the door. Her children were already at the bottom of the staircase, and every one of them would probably have been crushed to death, had she not put herself before the entrance and resisted the intruders. Major Harnage's wife, a Mrs. Raynell, the wife of the good lieutenant who had, on the preceding day, shared his soup with her, the wife of the commissary, and herself, were the only officers' wives at present with the army. They sat together, deploring their situation, when somebody having entered, all her companions exchanged looks of deep sorrow,—whispering at the same time to one another. She immediately suspected that her husband had been killed. She shrieked aloud, but was immediately told that nothing had happened to her husband, and was given to understand by a sidelong glance, that the lieutenant had been killed. His wife was soon called out, and found that the lieutenant was still alive, though one of his arms had been shot off, near the shoulder, by a cannon ball. They heard his groans and lamentations during the whole night, which were dreadfully reechoed through the vaulted cellar; and in the morning he expired.

Her husband came to visit her during the night, which served to diminish her sadness and dejection in some degree. On the next morning they thought of making their cellar a more convenient residence. Major Harnage and his wife, and Mrs. Reynell, took possession of one corner, and transformed it into a kind of closet, by means of a curtain. She was to have a similar retreat; but she preferred to remain near the door, that she might escape more easily in case of fire. She had straw put under her mattresses, and on these she laid herself with her children; and her female servants slept near them. Opposite to them were three officers, who though wounded, were determined not to remain behind if the army retreated. One of them was Captain Green, aid-de-camp to General Phillips, and a very amiable and worthy gentlemen. All three swore they would not depart without her in case of a sudden retreat, and that each of them would take one of her children on his horse. One of her husband's horses was constantly in readiness for herself. The Baron de Reidesel thought often of sending her to the American camp, to save her from danger; but she declared that nothing would be more painful to her than to live on good terms with those whom he was fighting; upon which he consented that she should continue to follow the army. However, the apprehension that he might have marched away, repeatedly intruded itself into her mind; and she crept up the staircase, more than once, to confirm or dispel her fears; and when she saw their soldiers near their watch-fires, she became more calm, and even could have slept.

The want of water continuing to distress them, they could not but be extremely glad to find a soldier's wife so spirited as to fetch some from the river, an occupation from which the boldest might have shrunk, as the Americans shot every one who approached it. They told them afterwards, she says, that they spared her on account of her sex.

She endeavored to dispel her melancholy by continually attending to the wounded. She made them tea and coffee, for which she received their warmest acknowledgements. She often shared her dinner with them. One day a Canadian officer came creeping into their cellar, and was hardly able to say that he was dying with hunger. She felt happy to offer him her dinner, by eating which he recovered his health and she gained his friendship. On their return to Canada she became acquainted with his family.

She also took care of Major Bloomfield, who was wounded by a musket ball, which passed through both his cheeks, knocked out his teeth and injured his tongue. He could retain nothing in his mouth, and soup and liquor were his only nourishment. Fortunately the Baroness had some Rhenish wine, and in the hope that the acidity would contribute to heal the wound, she gave him a bottle, of which he took a little now and then, and with such effect that he was soon cured. She thus acquired a new friend, and enjoyed some happiness in the midst of care and sufferings, which otherwise would have weighed heavily upon her spirits. On one of these mournful days, General Phillips, wishing to pay her a visit, accompanied her husband, who came once or twice daily at the risk of his life; and seeing their situation, and observing the entreaties she made to her husband not to be left behind, in case the army should suddenly break up, and her reluctance to fall into the hands of the Americans, he plead her cause, and said, on retiring, "I would not, for ten thousand guineas, see this place again. I am heart broken at what I have seen."

All their companions, however, did not deserve so much commisseration. They had some, she said, in their cellars who ought not to have been there, and who afterwards, when they were prisoners, were in perfect health, and walked about quite erect, and struted as much as they could. They remained six days in this doleful retreat. At last a capitulation was talked of, in consequence of having lost by useless delays, the opportunity of effecting their retreat. A cessation of hostilities took place, and her husband, who was quite exhausted by fatigue, could now, for the first time sleep quietly in a little chamber, while she retired with her children and the maid servants into the adjoining room. Towards one o'clock, she says a person came and asked to speak with him. She was very reluctant to awaken him at that hour of the night; and she soon observed that the errand did not much please him, for he immediately sent the messenger back to head-quarters, and laid himself down again out of humor. Soon after this General Burgoyne sent for all the Generals and field-officers, to attend a counsel of war early next morning, when he proposed to break the capitulation, in consequence of some groundless information he had received. It was however decided that this step was neither advisable nor practicable; and this determination was very fortunate for them, as the Americans told them afterwards, she says, that had they broken the treaty, they would all have been cut to pieces. This they could easily have done, as the British army was reduced to about five thousand men, while they had given the Americans time to raise their's to about fourteen thousand. On the morning of the 16th, however, her husband was obliged to repair to his post, and she to her cellar.

On the 17th of October the capitulation was carried into effect. The Generals waited upon the American General, Gates, and the troops surrendered themselves prisoners of war, and laid down their arms. The time had now come for the good woman, who had risked her life to supply them with water, to receive the reward of her services. Each of them threw a handful of money into her apron, and she thus received more than twenty guineas. At such a moment, at least, if at no other, the heart easily overflows with gratitude. When the Baroness drew near the tents, a good looking man, she says, advanced towards her, and helped the children from the calash, and kissed and caressed them; he then offered her his arm, and tears trembled in her eyes. "You tremble," said he, "do not be alarmed I pray you." "Sir," cried she, "a countenance so expressive of benevolence, and kindness which you have evinced towards my children, are sufficient to dispel all apprehensions." He then ushered her into the tent of General Gates, whom she found engaged in friendly conversation with Generals Burgoyne and Phillips. General Burgoyne said to her, "you can now be quite free from apprehension of danger." She replied that she should indeed be reprehensible if she felt any anxiety when their General felt none, and was on such friendly terms with General Gates.

The gentleman who received her, she says, with so much kindness, came and said to her "you may find it embarrassing to be the only lady in such a large company of gentlemen; will you come with your children to my tent, and partake of a frugal dinner, offered with the best will?" "By the kindness you shew to me," returned she, "you induce me to believe that you have a wife and children." He informed her that he was General Schuyler. He regaled her, she says, with smoked tongue, which were excellent, with beef-steaks, potatoes, fresh butter, and bread. Never did a dinner, she says, give so much pleasure as this. She was easy, after many months of anxiety; and there was the same happy change in those around her. That her husband was out of danger, was a still greater cause of joy to her. After their dinner, General Schuyler begged her to pay him a visit, at his house near Albany, where he expected that General Burgoyne would also be his guest. She sent to ask her husband's directions, who advised her to accept the invitation. As they were two days journey from Albany, and it was now near five o'clock in the afternoon, General Schuyler wished her to endeavor to reach on that day a place distant about three hours ride. He carried his civilities so far as to solicit a well bred French officer to accompany her on that first part of her journey.

On the next day, they reached Albany, where they so often wished themselves; but they did not enter that city, as they hoped they should, with a victorious army. The reception, however, which they met with from General Schuyler, his wife and daughters, was not like the reception of enemies, but of the most intimate friends. They loaded them, she says, with kindness; and they behaved in the same manner towards General Burgoyne, though he had ordered their splendid establishment to be burnt, and without any necessity, as it was said. But all their actions proved, that at the sight of the misfortunes of others, they quickly forgot their own. General Burgoyne was so much affected by this generous deportment, that he said to General Schuyler, "you are too kind to me who has done you so much injury." "Such is the fate of war," replied he, "let us not dwell on this subject." The Baroness remained three days with that excellent family, and they seemed to regret her departure.

As the reader may, possibly, have some desire to know how the author came to be living on the hallowed ground of "Bemis's Heights," and what *he* knows about the war, and Burgoyne, and Gates, and the marches and countermarches of the British and

APPENDIX 275

American armies, and when and where the battles were fought, and perhaps a thousand other notions, I will try to tell him,—*in my own way*.

My father, the late John Neilson, Esq. deceased, was born in Elizabethtown, or Amboy, or somewhere else, in the state of New-Jersey, on the 23d day of March, 1753, according to his own story, and he was always considered to be a man that followed the strict and straight forward line of truth. *His* father, and according to the legitimate line of *ascent*, *my* grandfather, Samuel Neilson, was an Englishman by birth, but whether he was uncle, or cousin, or any thing else to "My Lord"—Horatio Nelson, or by transposition, *Honor est a Nilo*, (for *he* fought the great battle of the Nile, and by his indomitable spirit of perseverance was I do not know, as I never have, very *scrutinizingly*, traced the line any farther back than to find out who was my *grandfather;* but this I know, or, at least, have been so informed, that he was a man of great resolution and uncommon perseverence, and so was *Lord* Nelson, and for that reason, as the same spirit runs down along the stream of family descent, I should be inclined to think there was some relationship, or some other *ship*, if it was not for that little *i* that seems to have intruded itself into the name of my grandfather, and so down along. But, as all things, especially in the natural world, are to be accounted for in some way or other, I will *try* to account for it in this way. We know there are some men who do not depend upon *ifs*, for instance, "*if* you will assist me I will do this, or try to do that," but rely altogether on their own strength and resolution, when about to execute some deed of valor, or requiring great mental exertion; and on that account, the pronoun *I* instead of the conjunction *if,* is more commonly used by them, as, *I* will do this, or *I* will do that, or "*I* will take the responsibility," and which may have been the fact in this case, and possibly, during a long voyage (for they had no steam-boats at that time) in crossing the Atlantic, the *I* may have forgotten its proper place, and accidentally slipped itself *into* the name, instead of taking its former position as a prefix. If that fact could be satisfactorily ascertained, and the result prove my reasoning to be true, why then, I should of course, from the circumstances before mentioned, and the fact of the same pronunciation being retained, claim, at least some *distant,* relationship to *"My Lord"* Nelson. But, until that question is settled, I shall, from necessity, be compelled to leave the reader to draw his own conclusion, while I go on and tell him something about my *grandmother,* on my father's side. Her name before she was married, for she too, my *fair* young readers, was once a maid, was Mary Courtenay, cousin (here I claim a relationship) to Lord Courtenay, well known in revolutionary times, and was born in the city of Dublin, but at what period of the world I do not now recollect, if I ever knew. She was a woman of strong and retentive memory, and endowed with an unconquerable passion for reading, and would often, when I was a little boy, call me and my little brothers and sisters into her room (for she lived with my father till she died,) and entertain us with long and numerous stories, about the wars, and the Indians, and how her second husband, my step-grandfather, was killed and scalped by them, and about her own sufferings and deprivations; and when the "big tear" would roll down her cheek, I would cry too,—and what is it now, gentle reader, that is stealing from my eye as I am writing this?—for we are sympathising creatures the best way we can fix it. But all this does not answer the questions as I promised in the beginning; though, as there is some *Yankee* blood in me, as you may possibly find out hereafter, I must have my own way of coming at it. Well, my grandfather was on the "stage" at the time of the Rev. William Tenant, David Brainard, and many other worthies with whom he was acquainted, and often entertained them at his house; from which circumstance, I have drawn the conclusion, very naturally too, that he was a "*good* man," and delighted in entertaining, not only known friends, but "strangers" too. He was never rich, especially in the things of this world, but in easy and comfortable circumstances, until, by misfortune, he became reduced, and soon after died, leaving three children, two sons and a daughter, of whom my father was the youngest, being then about ten years of age; and who, by his industry and *perseverance,* assisted my grandmother in obtaining a comfortable living, until she was married to her second husband, about eight years after. When he was nineteen, being quite a robust, athletic youth, and the times growing hard where he lived, he took a notion, like many other resolute boys in those days, that he would migrate to some other part of the country, where wages were better, and land was cheap, and try to work himself into a small farm of his own, by the time he became marriageable, for boys often begin to think about it at that age, though many of them, especially in these times, with less forethought.

On the twenty-third day of March, 1772, being his birth day, a robust youth, with only a few shillings in his pocket, and an axe on his shoulder, which was all the property he then owned; his wardrobe consisting of one suit of common coarse cloth, made sailor fashion, and one spare shirt, was seen taking leave of his parents and friends, somewhere in the state of New-Jersey. Thus externally and poorly equipt, though well endowed with a good and firm resolution in the inner man, or rather boy, he pursued a reversed course to the Hudson, until he arrived within about one mile of Bemis's Heights, for they were so called even at that remote period. Coming across two young fellows, who were lounging upon a log by the side of the road, as it is very common even at this time, at that season of relaxation, on a warm "sun-shiny" day, and being somewhat fatigued with his long travel, he took a seat with them, in order to make some enquiries about the country, for he began to think by this time, that he had got nearly to the end of the world, and especially the inhabited part of it. While conversing with these fellows, who appeared to be as ignorant of the country as himself, for they too came from a distance and were seeking employment, a man, who some two years previous had moved, with his family, from the "Land of steady habits," came along; and having cut over a large fallow the summer before, and wishing to clear it off and fence it the ensuing season, was in search of a "good hand" to help him. On enquiring of these "youngsters" if they were seeking work, and they all answering in the affirmative, he soon made his selection, and the "lot" fell upon the "New-Jersey boy," as possessing the greatest muscular strength, or at least, apparently so; and the axe too, that he brought so far on his shoulder, which in these times would have to be handled with gloves, was no *small* recommendation.

After very kindly directing the other two in the most advisable course to take, his employer, whose name (an odd one too) was Quitterfield, escorted him to his house, which was in sight, and it being near night, he was not set at work on that day.

The next morning he was up "bright and early," and there being no certain bargain made, unless on trial a few days, they should both be suited, his employer thought he would give him a fair one in the start. After breakfast, which was disposed of quite early, the old gentleman brought out his beetle and wedges, and having told John, for by this time some of the *gals*, (inquisitive creatures) had found out his name, he might split rails that day, he shouldered his axe, and catching up the other tools, they both started for the woods or fallow, some eighty rods from the house. On their arrival, the old gentleman led him up to a number of rail cuts which had been hauled together, and among them there was one "great big black-oak log," pretty considerable" winding, and told him he might commence on that. Having never split many rails, and eyeing the log sharply for a few moments, and examining both ends, he sprang upon the top of it, which raised him some three feet from "terra firma," and finding it very winding, he expressed some doubts whether it could be split, while there was as much frost in it as appeared to be at that time. The old gentleman, knowing from experience, that the task would be, at least a hard one, yet, as his principal object was to try the boy's "spunk," as he termed it, he rather insisted upon his making a thorough trial; and having very doubtingly in his own mind, encouraged him in the undertaking, returned to the house. After preparing two or three wooden wedges, or gluts as they are usually called, the youth pulled off his roundabout, or sailor coat, and commenced operations, with a full determination to *try* to perform any reasonable act that his employer might require of him. After hammering away for some time on the iron wedges, which would often fly back again, on account of the frost in the log, he at last, by constant friction, got them so heated, that they began to melt the frost, and consequently to "stay put." By this time the sweat beginning to start freely, he pulled off his jacket, and went at it again with more courage, or hopes of success, and mauled away until he drove them, with much difficulty up to their heads, before the log began to crack, when it started some two or three feet with a sound like the bursting of a twelve pounder. The sweat now running down his face, and into his eyes, like streams of liquid fire, he threw off his old hat, and wiping away the sweat with his shirt sleeve, prepared himself with much resolution, for a further and desperate encounter.

Having drove all the iron wedges up to their hilts, (heads I mean,) then came on the "tug of war" with the gluts, upon which he mauled and mauled, with a power not to be equalled by any son of Vulcan, until the sweat, in streams, ran off his face, and his clothes became saturated with the briny fluid; but at last bang! went the log, and the fur flew, or rather the bark, like chips from a turning lathe, when it opened some three or four feet further.

Now came on the closing scene, or "finis coronat opum." After "taking breath" a few moments, and a faithful application of the shirt slave, already drenched to its fill, and having placed the other gluts in the crevis or opening, he again went at it with renewed courage, and redoubled resolution, mauling away until their heads were mangled into brooms; but he still kept on, tugging, panting, and mauling, and the slivers snapping and cracking, and bark flying, when all at once, just as the horn was blowed for dinner, cr—ash! bang!! again went the *"great, big black-oak log,"* and fell apart, with a sound resembling some mighty explosion, and much to the joy of the young probationer.

He now, for the last time, applied the shirt sleeve, and having slipped on his hat and jacket, went whistling down to dinner, much elated with his success. As he entered the house, the old gentleman, who had something of a jovial turn, rather laughing in his sleeve, as the saying is, inquired, "Well, John, how many rails have you split?" He replied, with an arch smile, he had not counted them, but would before he came in at night, when the subject was dropped. After he had taken his dinner, and a few "sly winks," *perhaps,* had passed between him and some of the "gals," for there were some two or three of them, he returned to his beetle and wedges, and soon slivered the two halves into rails, and with the others he split that afternoon, he counted two hundred at night, and made his report accordingly. The old gentleman was not only much gratified with, but even disappointed at the number; for he did not suppose that he could have opened the first log, but had put him on it by way of trying his "grit" as he termed it. Being well satisfied with his first day's work, and the family with his deportment, and deeming any further trial unnecessary, a bargain was closed for the season. The summer passed away very satisfactorily, and with much inter-change of kind feelings, especially between *some* of the parties interested.

The time having arrived, though with more or less reluctance, perhaps, to a *certain* portion of the family, when his term of service was to expire, he left for some other place in the vicinity, though not without *occasional* calls "for old acquaintance sake." Thus matters passed along for about two years, and this New-Jersey boy had collected, by *"little crumbs,"* sufficient, with a trifling indulgence in credit, to purchase a small farm or piece of land on Bemis's Heights, on which, by his skill and industry he erected a "log cabin." Having cleared a small patch, sufficient to raise his own "turnips and cabbage," and about the same time, the eldest daughter of Mr. Quitterfield becoming, by mutual consent, Mrs. Neilson, the log cabin was soon occupied, and the premises, though much enlarged, have remained in the family ever since.

As the reader, no doubt, by this time begins to mistrust all the why's and wherefore's about the Author, and Bemis's Heights, and Battles, and Battle-ground, I may as well answer the questions at once, by saying, it was altogether owing to the *skill* and *perseverance* of the New-Jersey boy, in splitting that *"great, big, winding, black-oak log."*

And now gentle reader, both male and female, as this is my *first,* I'll promise you faithfully, it shall be my *last* attempt at "book-making;" and had it not been for that *"indomitable spirit of perseverance,"* that has been floated down to me, on the long stream of legitimate descent, from the remotest generation bearing the name, I should, before I got half through with *this,* have "cut stick" and run,—and many, perhaps, would have thanked me for it.

THE AUTHORS,
JOHN C. GREEN,
A. B. G.

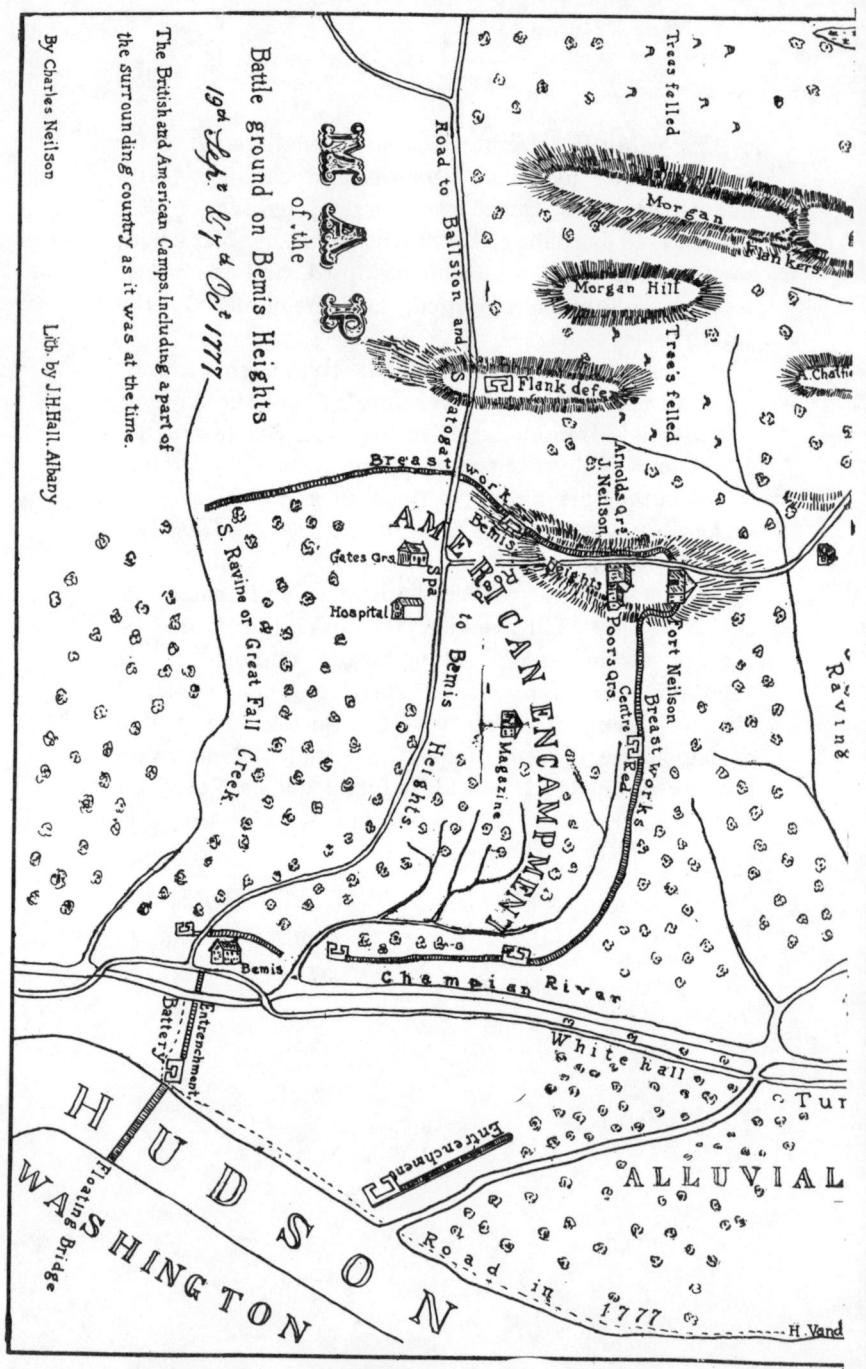

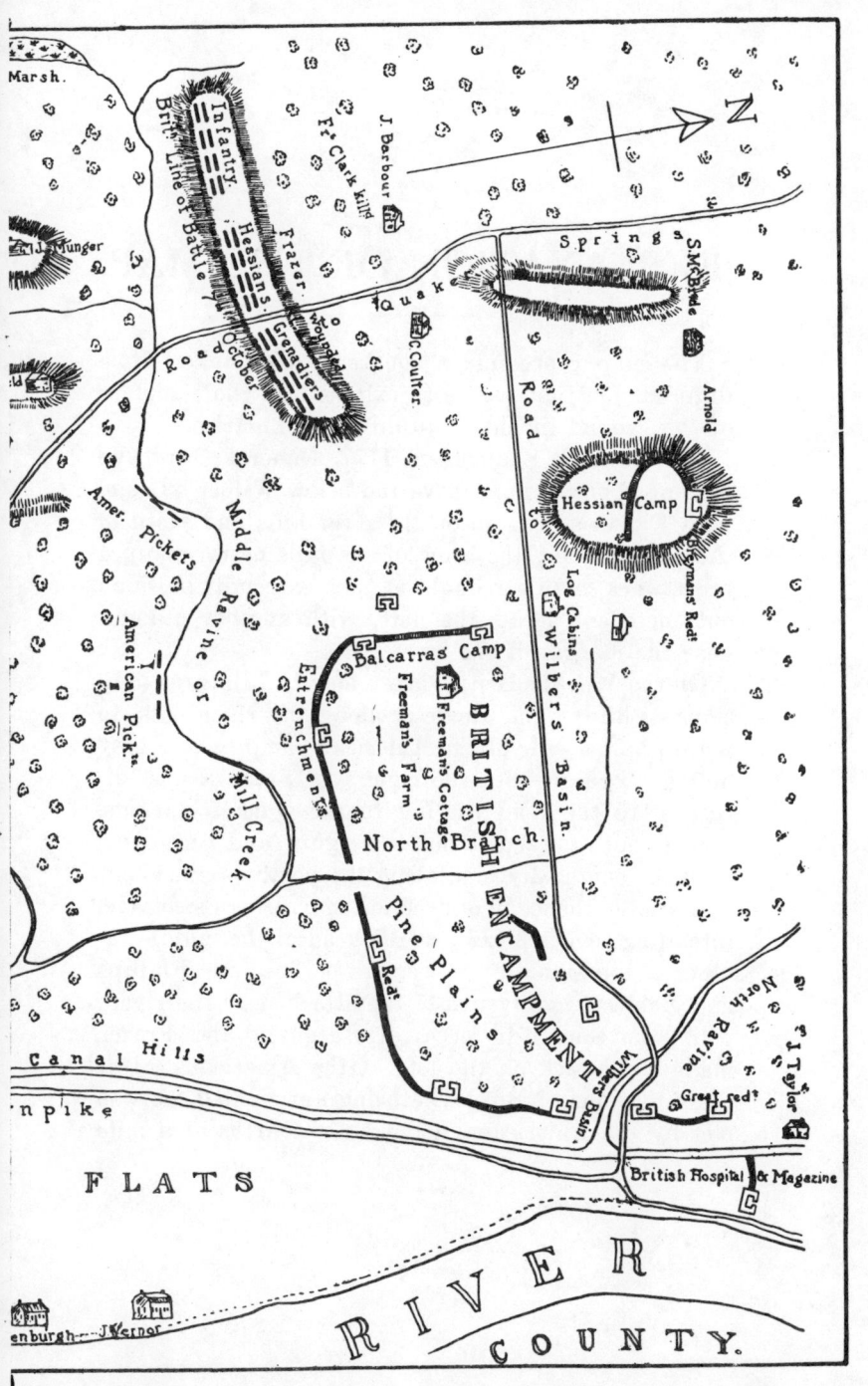

EXPLANATION OF THE MAP.

The map represents a southeast view taken from different positions, so as to exhibit the whole surface of the ground included within its boundaries.

On the 18th September, 1777, General Burgoyne encamped on the flats above and below Wilber's Basin, with Frazer's division on the river hills and plain in the rear. Along the brow of the hills he threw up a breastwork, with a redoubt at each extremity; also an entrenchment across the flats, with another redoubt near the margin of the river.

On the 19th the British army marched in three divisions—Phillips and Reidesel along the river flats, to within half a mile of the American camp, where they halted. Frazer, with the right wing, took a west direction to the road leading to the Quaker Springs, thence south towards Bemis's Heights; and Burgoyne, with the center division, along the north ravine about half a mile, thence in a direction to Freeman's cottage, intending to join Frazer at the head of the middle ravine, where signal guns were to be fired for Phillips and Reidesel to advance to the attack near the river; while the combined forces of Burgoyne and Frazer made the attack on the left of the Americans. But the intentions of Burgoyne being anticipated, he was met by the Americans, about three-fourths of a mile in advance of their lines, and before the junction took place. Consequently, the left wing, under Phillips and Reidesel, fell back from their advanced position, and on their retreat set fire to E. Vandenburgh's house, which was consumed.

At the commencement of the action on the 19th, General Frazer posted one thousand men on the rise of ground about one hundred and fifty rods north of west from Freeman's cottage, and advanced with five hundred to reinforce Burgoyne, whose division was already attacked. On Frazer's advance, he was met by Arnold at the head of his troops, in an open wood about sixty rods west of the cottage, where a severe engagement took place. Fearing that Arnold would cut him off from the main division under Burgoyne, which was his intention, Frazer brought on reinforcements from those troops posted on the high ground, alread mentioned, when Arnold, after obstinately contesting the ground for more than one hour, was compelled to retire, leaving the field literally drenched with human gore; and in some places, I have been informed by those who were in the action, the blood was ancle deep.

"Freeman's Farm," as it is usually called, where the general action was fought on the 19th September, was an oblong clearing in front of the cottage; its length extending east and west, and containing some twelve or fourteen acres of ground. At the eastern extremity of this clearing, the first gun was fired on that day, by a small scouting party, which had been sent out by General Gates to watch the movements of

Burgoyne on his advance, and who were there met by
a party of Canadians and Indians. The Americans,
being few in number, fled after the first fire, and the
Canadians and Indians, probably fearing an ambuscade, declined pursuit.

The skirmish on the flat bordering on Mill creek,
was near where that stream emerges from the river
hills. The place where it is said the Canadians and
Indians after being reinforced, entered the American
breastwork, which was then only partially completed,
was about forty rods west of the redoubt at the northeast angle of the camp.

After the battle of the 19th, Burgoyne, seeing the
impracticability of dislodging the Americans from
their entrenched position, established his magazine
and hospital near Wilber's Basin, where he encamped
on the 18th, and extended his line of fortifications,
from the river hills south of the north or great ravine,
across the plains west, to a point a little south of
Freeman's cottage, thence north and northwest to
Breyman's hill.

After the action of the 19th, the Americans completed their fortifications, which had already been laid
out, as designated on the map; and picket guards
were posted at different positions along the south bank
of Mill creek, or middle ravine, and on the rise of
ground near A. Chatfield's house; and also a line of
pickets along the ravine south of Mill creek, and between that stream and the camp.

The fifteen hundred men with Frazer at their head,
that first marched out of the British camp on the 7th

of October, were posted near the northern extremity of a rise of land near J. Munger's house, and named in the "Narrative" as the "right advance;" but previous to the action, five hundred of them were withdrawn, and formed a part of the right wing of the British line of battle. Colonel Morgan having posted his men on two hills, as designated on the map, made the attack in front and flank on the "right advance" of the British, and drove them in a northwest direction, to a swamp or marsh, where about two hundred were separated from the main body, and pursued by about as many of the riflemen, to about eighty rods west of J. Barber's house, where the British troops, being too hard pressed, ceased firing and "took to their heels." The riflemen then returned to the main body, which had just commenced a vigorous attack on the flank of the British light infantry.

In about fifty minutes after the action commenced, the British troops were driven in from all quarters, and were huddled together, like a flock of sheep, about sixty rods north of the center of their first position, and the Americans pouring in their deadly fire on three sides of them, at which time General Frazer was mortally wounded.

About the same time, General Ten Broeck came on the field, with about three thousand New York militia, and Burgoyne having lost many of his principal officers, and fearing he might be surrounded, ordered a retreat, when the British troops fled, like passengers out of an omnibus (at the tail end) to their entrenchments. General Learned, with a strong force, was directed to intercept them; but taking too large a circuit through a piece of woods, the British got in advance of him.

Both actions, namely, on the 19th September and 7th of October, commenced at the middle ravine; the first in a direct line between the fort on the Heights and Freeman's cottage; and the second, about twenty rods farther up, when the American picket was driven in.

At the close of the battle on the 7th October, the British were driven to their camp on the plains, east of the ravine branching off to the north from Mill creek. During the night, they broke up their camp on the plains, and retreated to their camp north of Wilber's basin, and in rear of their magazine and hospital.

All the dwellings included on the map were log cabins, except those of J. Neilson, E. Woodworth, J. Bemis, E. Vandenburgh, J. Vernor, and J. Taylor, (the Smith house, which now stands near the river.) This house was occupied, a portion of the time, by Burgoyne, as his head quarters, and also by the Baroness Reidesel and other ladies attached to the British army. It is also the house in which General Frazer died.

The farm owned by Joshua Barber, on which a part of the British line of battle was formed on the 7th October, is now owned by John Wilker, an aged and respectable member of the society of Friends, a good neighbor and a kind friend, who takes much delight in recounting the stories he has heard of the ever memorable battles on Bemis's Heights.

APPENDIX 289

General Arnold quartered in a log cabin which stood about three rods north of J. Neilson's house, and General Lincoln, after the battle of the 19th September, in J. Bemis's house.

The kitchen part of my dwelling, in which General Poor and Colonel Morgan quartered, being then in two rooms, is the only house now standing in which any of the American officers quartered at the time the army lay at Bemis's Heights. And the Smith house, then owned by John Taylor of Albany, and occupied by Billy M'Gee as tenant, previous to the approach of Burgoyne, and which, I regret to say, is now in the act of being demolished, is the last remaining one in which any of the British officers quartered.

The trees on the map are intended to represent that portion of land which was covered with wood at the time; and the other marks to represent the clearings or cultivated part.

The distance from Bemis's Heights to Ballston Spa, and Saratoga Springs, is twelve miles; to the Quaker Springs, which are also mineral waters, three and a half miles; to Stillwater Village three and a half miles; to Do-ve-gat, (which is the Dutch of cove,) seven miles; and to Saratoga (Schuylerville) ten miles.

Bemis's Heights, (proper) where the left wing of the American army was posted, and on which now stands the venerable mansion of the late John Neilson, Esq., deceased, is a gentle rise of ground, in the midst of quite an extended plain, and commanding the most beautiful, picturesque, and extensive landscape, to be found, perhaps, in the Empire State; having, as it were, at its foot, the meandering Hudson, the Champlain canal, and the Whitehall turnpike; the extensive range of Kaatsbergs and Helderbergs, with a broad expanse of country, in full prospect in front; Lake George mountains and their neighboring summits, in plain view in the rear; the long line of Green mountains, with a delightful intervening prospect, including Bennington heights, on the left; and a beautiful, variegated and extensive landscape on the right; which, being connected as it is, with its Revolutionary reminiscences, renders it a most eligible situation for a country seat, and well worthy of a visit from the admiring tourist, or the *earnest* attention of some gentleman of fortune.

History sheds a deeper interest over no portion of our beloved country. He who venerates the virtues and valor, and commiserates the sufferings of our fathers, and he who views with gratitude and reverence, the deliverances which Heaven has wrought for this land, will tread with awe on every foot of ground included within the boundaries of the accompanying map.

ERRATA

Page 5—4th line from top, omit the word *own*.
" 5—5th " for "mintue" read *minute*.
" 15—2d " for "minister" read *ministers*.
" 48—21st " for "prattlet" read *prattler*.
" 125—21st " for "his" read *the*.
" 160—14th " for "leaders" read *leader*.
" 179—19th " for "reach" read *reached*.
" 236—13th " for "reconnosance read *reconnoisance*.
" 237—9th " for "the" read *a*.
" 279—14th " omit the word *it*.
" 282—12th " for "slave" read *sleeve*.